REMEMBER
THE SABBATH

WHAT THE NEW TESTAMENT SAYS ABOUT
SABBATH OBSERVANCE FOR CHRISTIANS

DAVID WILBER

Remember the Sabbath: What the New Testament Says About Sabbath Observance for Christians

Pronomian Publishing LLC
Clover, SC 29710

ISBN: 979-8-9851529-1-3

Cover design: Jeromy Kusch (www.lanternministry.org)

"David Wilber's *Remember the Sabbath* is a thorough exegetical study of the Sabbath in the New Testament. Using a detailed contextual analysis of the Sabbath passages in the New Testament, David makes a strong case for the relevance of the Sabbath commandment for Jewish and Gentile believers alike. This book is written from a Christian perspective with an emphasis on answering common objections and questions related to practical observance of the Sabbath. Diligent students of Scripture will greatly benefit from this thought-provoking book."

Dr. Igal German, Moody Theological Seminary, Yesod Bible Center, and International Biblical Apologetics Association

"*Remember the Sabbath* provides an effective introduction to the historical and theological aspects of the Sabbath. David's arguments are logical and thorough, and he provides excellent resources for further study. For anyone looking into the question of whether Christians should consider the Sabbath, this book is an invaluable resource."

Mark Jacob, 119 Ministries

"In our day of Messianic restoration, many Believers have been convicted of the significant importance of God's Torah. An integral part of the Torah is the seventh-day Sabbath, embodied in the Fourth Commandment. Today's world—and especially the Body of Messiah—needs a day of rest! In a very uplifting and explorative way, David Wilber takes you on a journey of how he came to the conclusion that the Sabbath is an important institution that all of God's people need to be seriously considering. I am both humbled and encouraged to see that my teachings and writings have played a role in his journey. I sincerely hope that *Remember the Sabbath* is able to make a positive contribution to the growth and stability of the unique work that the Lord is doing in this hour!"

J.K. McKee, Messianic Apologetics and Outreach Israel Ministries

REMEMBER
THE SABBATH

**WHAT THE NEW TESTAMENT SAYS ABOUT
SABBATH OBSERVANCE FOR CHRISTIANS**

DAVID WILBER

CONTENTS

SHOULD WE REMEMBER THE SABBATH?

"The law of the ten commandments is strictly just ... It is a perfect
law, in which the interests of God and man are both studied."
— Charles Spurgeon[1]

The Ten Commandments are foundational to Christianity. These commandments give us insight into who God is and what matters to him. They distinguish God's people from the secular world, giving us a standard of just and wise behavior. They form the basis for the rest of the Torah's (Law of Moses') moral teachings and describe how we can love God and our neighbor. They were not given as a way for us to earn salvation, but rather given as a guide for how we should live as saved people.

Few Christians would say that the Ten Commandments are irrelevant for today. For instance, Christianity maintains that we shouldn't steal, lie, commit adultery, etc. However, despite its wording, one of the Ten Commandments seems to have been forgotten: "Remember the Sabbath day, to keep it holy" (Exodus 20:8). God commanded that the

---

1   Charles H. Spurgeon, "God's Law in Man's Heart," *Spurgeon Center*. www.spurgeon.org.

Sabbath day be kept as a special day of rest. The earliest Christians kept this commandment. However, most modern Christians treat the seventh day of the week as just another day. Should Christians remember the Sabbath again?

Usually, this question is met with answers like the following: "Jesus and the apostles teach that the Sabbath is no longer important!" "We don't need to rest on the seventh day; believing in the Messiah and resting in his completed work is how we keep the Sabbath now!" "God changed the day of the Sabbath from the seventh day to the first day; Christians 'keep the Sabbath' by going to church on Sunday!" "The Sabbath was intended only for the Jews, not Christians!" Indeed, judging from these popular reactions, it seems that many Christians consider the Sabbath a non-issue. The Sabbath is just an Old Testament commandment given to an Old Testament people. Therefore, Christians no longer need to keep this commandment, at least not in a literal sense.

Personally, when I started doing research on the Sabbath years ago, I had some of the same objections that were expressed above. I was astonished to find just how little biblical support there was for dismissing or changing the Sabbath. I saw that the New Testament never did away with the Sabbath but instead affirmed its ongoing validity. I learned that the Sabbath's disappearance in Christianity happened gradually over centuries, long after the time of the apostles. After studying the Scriptures and considering the evidence honestly, I could no longer ignore this commandment. And when I started actually observing the Sabbath day, I could no longer live without it.

In this book, I argue that the Sabbath is still relevant to all who profess to be Christians today. We will see from the New Testament that those of us who are Christians can and should observe the Sabbath day. Additionally, we will address the common reasons given for neglecting the Sabbath day and clear up much of the confusion surrounding this biblical commandment. Finally, we will answer common questions about what it means to keep the Sabbath from a biblical perspective.

In the midst of our high-pressure, fast-paced culture, when it's easy to become consumed in life's toils, the Sabbath blesses us with the opportunity to recalibrate and reprioritize our lives around what matters most. We weren't created to work our lives away. God gave us the gift of rest. I hope this book will help you experience the gift of rest that God has provided.

CHAPTER 1

THE NEW TESTAMENT CASE FOR SABBATH OBSERVANCE

This book argues from the New Testament that Christians should observe the Sabbath. Why focus on the New Testament instead of the Old Testament? Because it is obvious that the Sabbath was an important thing for God's people to keep in the Old Testament. After all, one of the Ten Commandments is to rest on the seventh day (Exodus 20:8-11), which is a reminder of what God did after he finished creation (Genesis 2:2-3). God declared the Sabbath to be a permanent sign between him and his people, Israel (Exodus 31:13). The Prophets cite Israel's breaking of the Sabbath as one of the reasons that God brought judgment upon them (Jeremiah 17:19-27; Ezekiel 20) while keeping the Sabbath is said to bring blessing (Isaiah 58:13-14). The Prophet Isaiah anticipated a future universal observance of the Sabbath for all mankind in the world to come (Isaiah 66:23).

Again, there is no question that God expected his people to keep the Sabbath in the Old Testament. The question is, did God's expectation for his people to keep the Sabbath change in the New Testament? Many Christians say yes. According to Christian theologian John MacArthur, "Jesus literally did away with the Sabbath."[1] However, is this statement in harmony with Scripture, or is it based on a misinterpretation of Scripture?

---

1   John MacArthur, "Understanding the Sabbath," *Grace to You*. www.gty.org.

In this chapter, we will look at some passages from the New Testament that affirm that Christians should continue to honor the Sabbath. Then, in the following chapters, we will examine the passages that seem to say the Sabbath is irrelevant to Christians or that it has changed. The goal will be to demonstrate that the New Testament is consistent in proclaiming the Sabbath's ongoing validity.

Matthew 5:17-20 — The Torah Upheld

When it comes to the question of whether Christians should keep the Sabbath, Yeshua's[2] words in Matthew 5:17-20 are worthy of our attention. The Sermon on the Mount (Matthew 5-7) explains how we are to live as members of the kingdom of heaven. Matthew 5:17-20 is a disclaimer of sorts that clarifies Yeshua's intentions regarding the Torah. As we will see, this passage has significant implications regarding the question of Sabbath observance.

Yeshua's sermon begins with the "Beatitudes" (Matthew 5:1-12), which are the blessings Yeshua proclaims upon all who accept the calling of kingdom life. The Beatitudes, according to Craig Keener, show us "what kingdom-ready people should be like."[3] This is followed by Yeshua's warning that if we fail to manifest these virtues, we become like salt that has lost its taste or a light that stays hidden (Matthew 5:13-15). In other words, if we do not live as kingdom members, we fail to impact the world for God's glory. Yeshua calls us to live as kingdom members so that others "may see your good works and give glory to your Father who is in heaven" (Matthew 5:16).

---

2   Throughout this book, I will be referring to Jesus by his Hebrew name, Yeshua, except for when I quote other sources.

3   Craig Keener, *The Gospel of Matthew: A Socio-Rhetorical Commentary* (Grand Rapids, MI: Eerdmans, 2009), 167.

How do we become salt and light to the world? What does it mean to live as members of the kingdom? Yeshua's Sermon on the Mount answers those questions. That answer begins with an important statement about the Torah and its role in the lives of Yeshua's followers:

> Do not think that I have come to abolish the Law or the
> Prophets; I have not come to abolish them but to fulfill them.
> —Matthew 5:17

In this passage, Yeshua emphatically declares that he did *not* come to abolish the Torah (Law) or Prophets. He says we are *not even to think* that he did such a thing. According to Noel Rabinowitz, Yeshua's command against wrong thinking in this regard has "a clear polemical and apologetic ring. Yeshua is here confronting the charge that he has abandoned the Torah of Moses."[4] Throughout the gospels, the scribes and Pharisees repeatedly accuse Yeshua and his disciples of abandoning the Torah (e.g., Matthew 12:1-14). Yeshua's statement here addresses those accusations directly. Again, he says that he did *not* come to abolish the Torah or Prophets and that we must not even *think* that he did.

What does Yeshua mean by the Torah and Prophets? The Torah and Prophets "is a traditional phrase referring to the Jewish Scriptures,"[5] that is, the Old Testament. So, what does Yeshua mean when he says that he did not come to *abolish* the Torah and Prophets? According to the BDAG lexicon, in this context, "abolish" (*kataluo*) means "to cause to be no longer in force...do away with, annul or repeal."[6] Thus, to

---

4   Noel Rabinowits, "Yes, the Torah is Fulfilled, But What Does This Mean?: An Exegetical Exposition," *Kesher* 11 (2000), 21.

5   Ibid.

6   Walter Bauer, *A Greek-English Lexicon of the New Testament and Other Early Christian Literature*, rev. and ed. Frederick W. Danker, 4th ed. (Chicago: University of Chicago

abolish *the Torah and Prophets*, according to Keener, means to "cast off its yoke, treating God's law as void."[7] That is, Yeshua did not come to nullify the authority of God's commandments in the Old Testament Scriptures.

Jewish literature from the first century AD confirms this meaning of *kataluo* ("abolish") in the context of abolishing the Torah.[8] For instance, 4 Maccabees 17:9 speaks of "the tyrant who wished to abolish the way of life of the Hebrews" in reference to Antiochus's attempt to prohibit Jews from observing the Torah during the time of the Maccabees. Moreover, 4 Maccabees 5 speaks of Antiochus trying to force the priest Eleazer to eat pork. Eleazer refuses because, from his perspective, eating unclean meat "abolishes" the Torah (4 Maccabees 5:33). Josephus also speaks of Antiochus's attempt to pressure the Jews "to abolish their ancestral customs" (*Wars of the Jews*, 1.34). These examples from first-century writings show that "abolishing the Torah" indicates stopping or discouraging obedience to the Torah's commandments. Yeshua reassures his hearers that he did *not* come to abolish the Torah's commandments.

So, what *did* Yeshua come to do? Instead of *repealing* or *doing away with* the Torah and Prophets, Yeshua said he came to "fulfill" them. This statement is a direct confirmation of the Torah's enduring validity—and by extension, the Sabbath's enduring validity. Yeshua came to affirm that the Torah's commandments remain relevant to his fol-

---

Press, 2021), 462.

7   Keener, *Matthew*, 177.

8   For an excellent study on how early Jewish literature informs our understanding of *kataluo* in Matthew 5:17, see Matthew Thiessen, "Abolishers of the Law in Early Judaism and Matthew 5,17-20." *Biblica* 93, no 4 (2012): 543-56.

lowers. As Carmen Imes puts it, "Jesus does not do away with the Old Testament law. He calls people back to it. And he holds them to it."[9]

In contrast to this view, some argue that to "fulfill" the Torah means to bring it to completion in the sense of prophetic realization, which then renders the Torah's commandments void.[10] According to Christian pastor Andy Stanley, "Jesus did not abolish the law when he fulfilled it. But in fulfilling it, he made it…obsolete."[11] Similarly, progressive Christian author Matthew Vines goes so far as to say, "Once Christ fulfilled the law, his followers would have trivialized his sacrifice by living as though they were still subject to the law's constraints."[12] Indeed, since the Messiah is the fulfillment of the Torah and Prophets—everything points to and culminates in him—the Torah is, as Andrew Schumacher puts it, "done away with by virtue of being fulfilled."[13] Thus, according to this interpretation, laws like the Sabbath no longer apply to Christians but only serve to point toward the Messiah.

It is true that the Messiah embodies the Torah in his actions and teachings, and his work on the cross certainly fulfills predictive proph-

9   Carmen Imes, *Bearing God's Name: Why Sinai Still Matters* (Downer's Grove, IL: InterVarsity Press, 2019), 143.

10 See R. L. Solberg, *Torahism: Are Christians Required to Keep the Law of Moses?* (Williamson College Press, 2019), 96: "Yeshua's sacrifice on the cross fulfilled what the Torah was pointing toward, and in doing so, rendered the Mosaic Covenant obsolete … [the Torah's] expiration date was the arrival of Christ … we are no longer bound by the legal requirements of the Law of Moses."

11 Andy Stanley, *Irresistible: Reclaiming the New that Jesus Unleashed for the World* (Grand Rapids, MI: Zondervan, 2018), 110.

12 Matthew Vines, *God and the Gay Christian: The Biblical Case in Support of Same-Sex Relationships* (Convergent Books, 2014), 199.

13 Andrew Schumacher, "Matthew 5 and the Hebrew Roots Movement, verse 17," *Beginning of Wisdom*. www.beginningwisdom.org.

ecies contained in the Torah and Prophets. However, in Matthew 5:17, "fulfill" does not convey prophetic realization.[14] First, the word "fulfill" (*pleroo*) is used in contrast with "abolish" (*kataluo*). As we have seen, according to the usages of *kataluo* in context with Torah that we find in first-century Jewish literature, "abolish the Torah" in Matthew 5:17 indicates repealing the Torah's commandants. It seems strange for Matthew to contrast the idea of repealing the Torah's commandments with the idea of fulfilling prophecy. A more natural contrast to the idea of repealing the Torah's commandments is the idea of *affirming* the Torah's commandments. Second, the immediate context indicates that Yeshua's coming to fulfill the Torah is demonstrated in how the Torah would be lived out. In verse 19, Yeshua admonishes his followers to do and teach the Torah's commandments. Because of these factors, in Matthew 5:17, "fulfill" is better understood as "bring to full expression=show it forth in its true [meaning]."[15] Instead of rendering the Torah's commands over and done away with, Yeshua came to confirm

---

14   Even if prophetic realization is the intended meaning of "fulfill" in Matthew 5:17, the idea that some laws are now repealed does not follow from that premise. See J.K. McKee *The New Testament Validates Torah: Does the New Testament Really Do Away With the Law?* (Richardson, TX: Messianic Apologetics, 2012), 276-277: "[E]ven if you choose to look at plēroō in v. 17 as exclusively pertaining to prophecy, to claim that the Torah's instructions get abolished in the process is not at all a tenable position. The Apostolic Scriptures, for example, affirm that Yeshua's sacrificial work has inaugurated the era of the New Covenant (Luke 22:20; Hebrews 8:8-12), yet the prophesied New Covenant involves a supernatural transcription of the Torah's commands onto the hearts of God's people (Jeremiah 31:31-34; Ezekiel 36:25-27). Likewise, at the proclamation of the Word of God, which can be viewed as the gospel, the nations will come to Zion to be taught the Law, ultimately resulting in worldwide peace (Isaiah 2:2-4; Micah 4:1-3). So, even if you argue from Matthew 5:17 that Yeshua came to only accomplish the prophetic predictions of the Torah and Prophets—the Torah is by no means to be considered relevant only for the pre-resurrection era."

15   BDAG, "πληρόω," 736.

them through his teachings and actions.[16] He came to bring the Torah to full expression by teaching and demonstrating how to properly live it out on the basis of love for God and one's neighbor. As J. Andrew Overman explains:

> Matthew's community understands, teaches, and does the law. This is the fulfillment of the law and the righteousness which surpasses that of the Matthean antagonists. If you not only teach the law but do it, applying the dominant principles of love and compassion, you have fulfilled the law and properly enacted the will of God in heaven (7:12; 12:50; 21:31). Love and mutuality, as seen in the antitheses, guide the interpretation of the valid and enduring law.[17]

Yeshua's Sermon on the Mount is all about bringing out the Torah's fullest and proper application and meaning.[18] That is what Yeshua means when he says he came to "fulfill" the Torah. While some read the

---

16   See Keener, *Matthew*, 177: "When Jesus says that he came not to 'abolish' the law and prophets but to 'fulfill,' he uses terms that would have conveyed his faithfulness to the Scriptures. To 'fulfill' God's law was to 'confirm' it by obedience and demonstrating that one's teaching according with it; to 'annul' it was to cast off its yoke, treating God's law as void."

17   J. Andrew Overman, *Matthew's Gospel and Formative Judaism: The Social World of the Matthean Community* (Minneapolis, MN: Fortress Press, 1990), 89.

18   See Donald A. Hagner, *Matthew 1-13: Word Biblical Commentary 33a* (Dallas, TX: Word, 1993), 106: "Since in 5:21-48 Jesus defines righteousness by expounding the true meaning of the law as opposed to wrong or shallow understandings, it is best for us to understand [*plerosai*] here as "fulfill" in the sense of "bring to its intended meaning"— that is, to present a definitive interpretation of the law, something now possible because of the presence of the Messiah and his kingdom. Far from destroying the law, Jesus' teachings—despite their occasionally strange sound—penetrate to the divinely intended (i.e., the teleological) meaning of the law."

"antitheses" in Matthew 5:21-48 ("you have heard it said…but I tell you") as Yeshua setting himself up in opposition to the Torah,[19] Yeshua's statement in Matthew 5:17 makes that interpretation impossible. In fact, the risk of that interpretation is the main reason Yeshua says, "Do not think…" in verse 17. He pre-emptively dispels the notion that his teachings are anti-Torah. His antithetical statements in Matthew 5:21-48, therefore, "flow from the opening statement on the enduring nature of the Law and Prophets."[20] He urges his followers to return "to the original intent of the Sinai instructions,"[21] a Torah observance guided by love and compassion. Yeshua doesn't overthrow the Torah; he explains it.[22]

Why is this important? Because Yeshua's affirmation of the Torah includes the Sabbath. Elsewhere in Matthew's gospel, we see the Messiah's own faithful observance of the Sabbath in addition to his teachings regarding what it means to keep it properly. Like his teachings on other laws in the Torah, the Messiah's teachings on the Sabbath address misunderstandings from his contemporaries and emphasize the original

---

19 See Andrew Schumacher, "Matthew 5 and the Hebrew Roots Movement, verse 19," *Beginning of Wisdom*. www.beginningwisdom.org: "[R]eading this section tells us one reason Jesus might have talked about not thinking He came to abolish the law. He spends a fair amount of time challenging the perceptions of His hearers concerning the law, enough that it may sound to some like He was issuing challenges to the law…His own commandments are being issued here."

20 Tim Hegg, "What Does Plerosai ('to fulfill') Mean in Matthew 5:17?" *ETS Annual Meeting* (Nashville, 2000), 18.

21 Imes, *Bearing God's Name*, 142.

22 See P.J. Hartin, "Ethics in the Letter of James, the Gospel of Matthew, and the Didache: Their Place in Early Christian Literature," *Matthew, James, and Didache: Three Related Documents in Their Jewish and Christian Settings* (Atlanta, GA: Society of Biblical Literature, 2008), 294: "Matthew's Jesus does not take issue with the Torah as such, for the Torah is God's expressed will. Instead, Matthew's Jesus claims the role as official interpreter of God's will, of God's Torah."

intent of the commandment. According to the Messiah, the Sabbath is a joyful day to glorify God by doing good (e.g., Matthew 12:9-13). Yeshua doesn't do away with the Sabbath; he "fulfills" it by demonstrating how to observe it properly.

The verses that follow Matthew 5:17, which are explanatory of Yeshua's opening statement that he came to fulfill the Torah and Prophets,[23] make it even clearer that the Torah, and therefore the Sabbath, remains valid and authoritative for Christians today:

> For truly, I say to you, until heaven and earth pass away, not an iota, not a dot, will pass from the Law until all is accomplished.
> —Matthew 5:18

In Matthew 5:18, Yeshua stresses the immutability of the Torah by stating emphatically that even the smallest details of it matter and remain intact. By *iota*, Yeshua refers to the Hebrew letter *yod*, the smallest letter in the Hebrew alphabet. The combination of *iota* and *keraia*

---

23 See Tim Hegg, "What Does Plerosai ('to fulfill') Mean in Matthew 5:17?" 6-7: "In good semitic fashion, Yeshua gives a summary or outline in His opening statement of the point He intends to make. The following lines, then, work to expand and explain the opening statement, further describing the negative, what Yeshua *did not come* to do, or the positive, *what Yeshua did come to do*. In the opening phrase, the negative is described in the word "destroy," while the positive is in the term "fulfill" ... Expanding the concepts of "abolish" and "fulfill," the following verses have (v. 18) "pass away," which aligns with "abolish," and "is accomplished," which corresponds to "fulfill." Likewise, in v. 19, "destroy" is parallel to "abolish" while "keeps" corresponds to "fulfill" ... This structure is obvious: "to abolish" is to cause aspects of the Law to pass away and thus to annul its affect and reality in the lives of people. Conversely, "to fulfill" is to see the commandments and precepts of the Torah and Neviim implemented in the lives of those waiting for the kingdom, paralleled by the word [keeps]."

(dot) "should be understood as an hendiadys meaning 'the smallest stroke of the smallest letter.'"[24] By using popular traditions within contemporary Jewish teaching of his time,[25] Yeshua underlines his point about the Torah's validity in the strongest of ways. As David Turner writes, "It would be hard to make a stronger statement of the ongoing authority of the Torah than that made in 5:18."[26] Every detail of the Torah, including the Sabbath, is essential according to the Messiah.

What did Yeshua mean when he said that nothing will pass away from the Torah "until heaven and earth pass away" and "until all is accomplished"? According to Donald Hagner, these statements refer to "the end of time as we know it and the beginning of eschatology proper, that is, the time of the regeneration of the created order."[27] This understanding suggests that the entire Torah remains binding and authoritative until the arrival of the new heavens and new earth, when the present created universe passes away (2 Peter 3:7, 13; Revelation 21:1).

In contrast to this view, some interpret the second clause ("until all is accomplished") as having already occurred. According to this interpretation, parts of the Torah can now be discarded.[28] However,

---

24 Tim Hegg, *The Gospel of Matthew: Chapters 1-7* (Tacoma, WA: TorahResource, 2007), 179.

25 See Keener, *Matthew*, 178: "[Jewish teachers] said that when Sarai's name was changed to Sarah, the yodh removed from her name cried out from one generation to another, protesting its removal from Scripture, until finally, when Moses changes Oshea's name to Joshua, the yodh was returned to Scripture. 'So you see,' the teachers would say, 'not even the smallest letter can pass from the Bible' (b. Sanh. 107ab; p. Sanh. 2:6, §2; Gen. Rab. 47:1; Lev. Rab. 19:2; Num. Rab. 18:21; Song Rab. 5:11, §§3-4)."

26 David L. Turner, *Matthew* (Grand Rapids, MI: Baker Academic, 2008), 163.

27 Hagner, *Matthew*, 108.

28 See Stanley, *Irresistible*, 111: "According to Jesus, nothing in the law would 'disappear' until everything was 'accomplished.' Once it was accomplished, however, the law would

New Testament scholars widely reject that interpretation. Keener says that such an interpretation "violates the whole thrust of the passage."[29] Overman likewise remarks, "Such hermeneutical gymnastics seem excessive, if not tortured."[30] The obvious problem with interpreting the second clause as referring to a separate earlier event (such as when Yeshua accomplished his work on the cross) is that it "plainly contradicts the meaning of the first clause, which refers to the ongoing validity of the law until the end of the age."[31] According to Hagner, the correct approach is to "take the clauses as essentially synonymous."[32] Thus, when Yeshua says that nothing from the Torah will pass away until all is accomplished, he means nothing from the Torah will pass away "until the consummation of the kingdom, when heaven and earth pass away."[33]

If not even "the smallest stroke of the smallest letter" of the Torah has passed away,[34] it is reasonable to see that neither has the Sabbath.

---

begin to disappear. Which is exactly what happened...God's covenant with Israel was no longer needed. It had been fulfilled and replaced with a better covenant."

29   Craig Keener, *Matthew*, 178.

30   J. Andrew Overman, *Church and Community in Crisis: The Gospel According to Matthew* (Valley Forge, PA: Trinity Press International), 77-78: "Such contrived interpretations of 5:17-20 are also a result of isolating these verses from the rest of the Gospel. Indeed, throughout the Gospel Matthew demonstrates a sophisticated knowledge of the law, its interpretation, and the abiding validity of the law as he interprets it ... Although this passage is the subject of lively controversy, it is unambiguous and does indeed command obedience to the whole Torah."

31   Hagner, *Matthew*, 107.

32   Ibid.

33   Keener, *Matthew*, 178.

34   Some have argued that this verse cannot mean what it plainly says because some parts of the Torah, like the laws governing the Levitical Priesthood and sacrifices, *have* passed away in light of the Messiah's work on the cross. But this is another misunderstanding of New Testament teaching. See chapter 5 under the heading, "Some parts of the Torah

The command to observe the Sabbath, as expressed in the Torah, remains valid instruction for God's people. It is among the commandments that Yeshua expects his followers to "do" and "teach," as we see in the next verse:

> Therefore whoever relaxes one of the least of these commandments and teaches others to do the same will be called least in the kingdom of heaven, but whoever does them and teaches them will be called great in the kingdom of heaven.
> —Matthew 5:19

Carrying forward his earlier teaching that his followers are to let their light shine before others through their good works (Matthew 5:14-16), here Yeshua admonishes his followers to be great in the kingdom of heaven by doing and teaching the Torah's commandments. Yeshua warns that whoever "relaxes" even the least of the commandments will be least in the kingdom. "Relaxes" is the Greek word *luo*, which is related to *kataluo*, the word translated "abolish" in verse 17. Like *kataluo*, *luo* in this context similarly carries the meaning of "repeal, annul, abolish."[35] Essentially, Yeshua says that since he did not come to repeal the Torah's commandments, neither should his followers. According to Keener, Yeshua's point in Matthew 5:19 "is the same as that of other Bible teachers in his day: one cannot pick and choose among the commandments but must obey them all."[36] If we want to be great in the kingdom of heaven, we must not brush-off even the least

---

have passed away, such as animal sacrifices and the Levitical priesthood. So, is it true to say that Matthew 5:18 affirms Sabbath observance?"

35   BDAG, "λύω," 538.
36   Keener, *Matthew*, 179.

commandment. All the commandments—including the Sabbath—are important, and none of them should be ignored.

Against this view, some try to argue that when Yeshua says "these commandments" in verse 19 that he is "referring to His own commandments that He is about to discuss in the sermon on the mount."[37] That is, Yeshua does not admonish his followers to do and teach the commandments of *the Torah* but instead *his own distinct commandments*. The "antitheses" in Matthew 5:21-48 ("you have heard it said... but I tell you") are often cited in support of this idea. However, is that understanding a proper reading of the text? According to Hagner, "in keeping with the emphasis of the preceding verses, ['the least of these commandments'] is more naturally taken as a reference to the Mosaic law, and the equivalent of the 'jot and tittle' of v 18."[38] A better explanation for some of the contrasting statements in Matthew 5:21-48 is that Yeshua is not opposing the Torah but rather the scribes' and Pharisees' teachings on the Torah. Contrary to the teachings of his contemporaries, Yeshua gives the *correct interpretation* of the Torah, drawing out the original intent of the commandments. As Hagner explains:

> By means of six bold antitheses representing the teaching of
> Jesus, Matthew now contrasts Jesus' exposition of the true
> and ultimate meaning of the Torah with the more common,
> rabbinic understandings of the commandments. In this way
> the incomparable ethical demands of the kingdom are set

---

37 Andrew Schumacher, "Matthew 5 and the Hebrew Roots Movement, verse 19," *Beginning of Wisdom*, www.beginningwisdom.org.

38 Hagner, *Matthew*, 108.

forth, and in this way examples are provided showing how the righteousness of the Pharisees is to be exceeded.[39]

Once again, nothing from the Torah is done away with. Yeshua clearly expects his followers to observe the commandments of the Torah, which includes the Sabbath. But our Torah observance, including our Sabbath observance, must be in accordance with the "true meaning of the Torah now delivered by the Messiah,"[40] as we see in the next verse:

> For I tell you, unless your righteousness exceeds that of the scribes and Pharisees, you will never enter the kingdom of heaven.
> —Matthew 5:20

Here Yeshua calls his followers to a way of righteousness that exceeds the scribes and Pharisees. In context, this "righteousness" refers to "the manner in which obedience to the Torah is manifest by one's actions."[41] In other words, Yeshua says that his followers' Torah observance must be better than the scribes' and Pharisees' Torah observance. But how do Yeshua's followers observe the Torah better than the scribes and Pharisees?

First, unlike the scribes and Pharisees who preach but do not practice the Torah's commandments (Matthew 23:3), Yeshua's followers must actually teach *and do* the commandments (Matthew 5:19). Second, sometimes the scribes and Pharisees nullified explicit commandments of the Torah through their traditions and reinterpretations

---

39   Ibid., 111.
40   Ibid., 109.
41   Hegg, *Matthew*, 186.

(e.g., Matthew 15:1-9). Therefore, Yeshua's followers must affirm God's word as the ultimate authority. Third, Yeshua's followers must observe the Torah in accordance with the teachings and example of the Messiah. Yeshua gives the definitive interpretation of the Torah, a Torah observance guided by love and compassion.

When it comes to the Sabbath specifically, our Sabbath observance will exceed that of the scribes and Pharisees when we 1) not just teach but also *do* the Sabbath, 2) uphold God's word, not men's teachings, as the final authority on matters pertaining to the Sabbath, and 3) observe the Sabbath in accordance with the teachings and example of the Messiah. Like the prophets in the Old Testament (e.g., Isaiah 58:13), Yeshua spoke against the distortions of the Sabbath of his day and called for a return to genuine Sabbath observance in accordance with God's will. We will see how Yeshua's teachings regarding the Sabbath contrast with the Pharisees' teachings in the next chapter.

Some say it is incorrect that Yeshua affirms Torah observance in Matthew 5:17-20 because that would mean that Torah observance grants us entry into the kingdom.[42] Obviously, the idea that Torah observance gets us into the kingdom contradicts the biblical doctrine of salvation by grace through faith (Ephesians 2:8). But Yeshua isn't saying that entrance into the kingdom is based on our own righteousness; rather, he says that members of the kingdom will be righteous. As Hagner explains:

---

42 See Andrew Schumacher, "Matthew 5 and the Hebrew Roots Movement, verse 20," *Beginning of Wisdom*. www.beginningwisdom.org: "Jesus is saying that the righteousness required to enter the kingdom is so high, that obedience to the law is a hopeless path to get there ... And if His point is not to point us to the law, but to Himself, it would make no sense to begin that argument by telling us to obey the law He is about to supersede in His sermon."

> The larger context of the verse (e.g., the grace of the beati-
> tudes) forbids us to conclude that entrance into the kingdom
> depends, in a cause-effect relationship, upon personal moral
> attainments. The verse is addressed, it must be remembered, to
> those who are the recipients of the kingdom. Entrance into the
> kingdom is God's gift; but to belong to the kingdom means to
> follow Jesus' teaching. Hence, the kingdom and the righteous-
> ness of the kingdom go together; they cannot be separated.
> And it follows that without this righteousness there can be no
> entrance into the kingdom (cf. 6:33).[43]

Yeshua's teaching here can be compared to the epistle of James. Some misunderstand James to be teaching works-based salvation because he says, "a person is justified by works and not faith alone" (James 2:24). But James doesn't deny that we are justified by faith. He doesn't teach that faith can't save us; he teaches that *counterfeit faith* can't save us. What is counterfeit faith? It is the kind of "faith" that doesn't lead to doing good works. James affirms that we are saved by faith, but faith needs to be defined correctly. Doing good works is the necessary outgrowth of saving faith.

Similarly, Yeshua's point in verse 20 is that genuine members of the kingdom of heaven—those who are saved by grace through faith by definition—will walk in righteousness. Our righteousness will exceed that of the scribes and Pharisees because it is based on Yeshua's ful-fillment of the Torah. In contrast to the scribes and Pharisees, Yeshua teaches a Torah observance on the basis of love for God and neighbor. He writes the Torah on the hearts of his followers, transforming them from the inside out, in accordance with the New Covenant promises

---

43   Hagner, *Matthew*, 109.

(Jeremiah 31:31-34; Ezekiel 36:25-27). We are granted membership into the kingdom by God's grace, but being a member of the kingdom means we now walk in righteousness in accordance with Yeshua's teachings on the Torah.

In summary, Yeshua said he came to fulfill the Torah—that is, confirm the Torah through his teachings and actions, demonstrating how to observe it properly. Nothing from the Torah will pass away until the future consummation of the kingdom when heaven and earth pass away. Followers of Yeshua are to do and teach even the least of the Torah's commandments in accordance with Yeshua's teachings, thereby surpassing the scribes and Pharisees in righteousness. The Torah includes the command to observe the Sabbath; therefore, Yeshua affirms the ongoing validity and authority of the Sabbath commandment in Matthew 5:17-20.

Mark 2:27 — The Sabbath Was Made for Man

While walking through a grain field on the Sabbath, Yeshua's disciples plucked handfuls of grain to eat. This act brought criticism from some Pharisees, who accused Yeshua's disciples of transgressing the Sabbath. Their accusation was baseless, as we will cover in-depth in the next chapter, but it is in this context that Yeshua makes a profound statement. He says, "The Sabbath was made for man, not man for the Sabbath" (Mark 2:27).

Yeshua's statement in Mark 2:27 expresses the Sabbath's universal and perpetual nature. He announces that God established the Sabbath in creation "for all people, not just those who are ethnically descended from Abraham."[44] Many scholars have recognized the implications of Yeshua's words:

---

44 Craig Keener, "Which day is the Sabbath?" *Bible Background: Research and Commentary*

What Jesus's choice of words seems to imply, therefore, is that when God made the world, he also made the Sabbath, and that he made it not just for Israel but for mankind. If so, he endorses the natural interpretation of Gen. 2:3, in the manner of Aristobulus and Philo, and declares the Sabbath, like marriage, to be a creation ordinance of general and permanent validity.[45]

By this memorable affirmation then, Christ does not abrogate the Sabbath commandment but establishes its permanent validity by appealing to its original creation when God determined its intended function for the well-being of mankind.[46]

It is clear that God instituted the Sabbath for all human beings on planet Earth because He instituted it in the beginning, long before Israel existed, along with basic elements of human life such as marriage and labor.[47]

As Jesus indicated pointedly, "the Sabbath came into being (*egéneto*) for the sake of man (*dià tòn anthrōpon*)" (Mark 2:27). Because it was for the good of man and the whole of creation, God instituted the Sabbath. Neither antinomianism nor

from Dr. Craig Keener, www.craigkeener.com.

45 Roger T. Beckwith, *Calendar and Chronology, Jewish and Christian: Biblical, Intertestamental and Patristic Studies* (Brill Academic Publishers, 2001), 16.

46 Samuele Bacchiocchi, *The Sabbath in the New Testament* (Berrien Springs, MI: Biblical Perspectives, 2000), 27.

47 Roy Gane, "Sabbath and the New Covenant," *JATS*, 10/1-2 (1999), 316.

dispensationalism may remove the obligation of the Christian today to observe the creation ordinance of the Sabbath.[48]

Yeshua's statement in Mark 2:27 reveals God's purpose for the Sabbath from the beginning. It was made for man's enjoyment. As we will explore in the next chapter, the Pharisees failed to uphold this purpose in their teachings. It seems strange that Yeshua would emphasize the true purpose of the Sabbath day if his intention was to repeal it. On the other hand, Yeshua's insistence on understanding the Sabbath's original purpose is precisely what we would expect if he considered the Sabbath to still be important.

In summary, Mark 2:27 states that the Sabbath was established in creation to benefit all mankind. The Sabbath was not given exclusively to Israel but was instituted before there even was an Israel. Yeshua's statement on the Sabbath's purpose implies that it is still relevant to all Christians today.

The Example of Yeshua and the Apostles

In light of his direct statements on the matter, did Yeshua's own behavior demonstrate that he considered the Sabbath valid? Luke records that it was Yeshua's custom to attend the synagogue services every Sabbath: "And he came to Nazareth, where he had been brought up. And as was his custom, he went to the synagogue on the Sabbath day, and he stood up to read" (Luke 4:16). As we see, Yeshua not only attended synagogue services on the Sabbath regularly but also participated in the public reading and teaching of Scripture. Yeshua's customary participation in the synagogue services is evident through-

---

48   O. Palmer Robertson, *The Christ of the Covenants* (Phillipsburg, NJ: Presbyterian and Reformed Publishing, 1980), 69.

out the gospels.[49] Moreover, in Matthew 24:20, Yeshua admonished his followers to pray that they wouldn't have to flee on the Sabbath during the coming tribulation.[50] If Yeshua intended to repeal the Sabbath commandment, we would not expect him to faithfully observe the Sabbath himself or express concern over his followers' ability to observe the Sabbath in the future.

What did the apostles' faith look like after Yeshua's ascension? Did they behave in a way that reflected a belief in the Sabbath's ongoing validity? In the book of Acts, we see that the apostles followed in their Messiah's footsteps by regularly attending and participating in the synagogue services on the Sabbath. For example, in Acts 13:13-52, we read that Paul traveled to Antioch and taught in the synagogue on the Sabbath. Paul taught both Jews and Gentiles about how Yeshua is the promised Messiah of the Hebrew Scriptures. Paul and Barnabas returned the following Sabbath to teach more (13:42, 44). In Acts 17, Paul traveled to Thessalonica and once again attended the synagogue services on the Sabbath. This was his "custom," according to Acts 17:2. In Acts 18, Paul traveled to Corinth, where we see him attending the synagogue services "every Sabbath," trying to persuade both Jews and Gentiles concerning the promised Messiah (Acts 18:4). In Acts 16, when Paul was in Philippi, no synagogue was available—but that didn't stop him from keeping the Sabbath! He and others gathered at a riverside to pray (Acts 16:13).

Some have tried to downplay these references to Paul attending synagogue on the Sabbath by suggesting that Paul's custom was a

---

49   Matthew 4:23; 9:35; Mark 3:1; 6:2; Luke 4:44; 6:6; 13:10; John 18:20.

50   For a more detailed explanation of the significance of this verse, see chapter 5 under the heading, "How should we understand Yeshua's comments about fleeing on the Sabbath in Matthew 24:20?"

mere missionary strategy to convert Jews to Christians, not part of his observance of the Sabbath. Arthur G. Patzia declares, "Contacts with the synagogue...were important in Paul's missionary activity only as opportunities to initiate the proclamation of the gospel."[51] However, this suggestion assumes that Paul and the other apostles believed they started some new religion, separate from Judaism, instead of seeing their faith as within the parameters of first-century Judaism. The earliest Christians were designated as the "sect of Nazarenes" (Acts 24:5). The word "sect" (*hairsesis*) is also used to describe the Pharisees (Acts 15:5) and Sadducees (Acts 5:17), which were both within broader Judaism in the first century. Thus, it really shouldn't surprise us that the earliest believers in Yeshua continued to meet in synagogues on the Sabbath. As faithful Jews, why wouldn't they? Denis Fortin puts it well:

> [W]hat Luke is describing is not Paul inviting Jews and
> Gentiles to form a new religion; rather, he is proclaiming the
> fulfillment of God's promise of a Messiah and this promise is
> for both Jews and Gentiles. Seen from this perspective, Paul's
> visits to synagogues on Sabbath are not merely a strategy to
> win converts. Paul can be seen as a faithful Jew and observing
> the Sabbath: at this point in early Christian history, Paul and
> his colleagues are Jewish believers in Jesus the Messiah and
> keep the Sabbath.[52]

---

51 Arthur G. Patzia, *The Emergence of the Church: Context, Growth, Leadership and Worship* (Downers Grove, IL: InterVarsity Press, 2001), 187.

52 Denis Fortin, "Paul's Observance of the Sabbath in Acts of the Apostles as a Marker of Continuity Between Judaism and Early Christianity," *AUSS* Vol. 40, No. 2 (2015), 329.

The apostles saw their faith in Messiah as the fulfillment of God's promises to Israel in the Hebrew Scriptures. They wanted to preach this good news to their fellow Jews (and God-fearing Gentiles), and the obvious place to reach their people was in the synagogue on the Sabbath. How convenient considering that the apostles, as faithful Jews, already attended Sabbath services regularly! Paul's intention was not to infiltrate the synagogue to pull people out of it, but rather "to worship with other Jews and to invite them to rejoice with him for what God has done in Jesus."[53]

What about the Gentiles who came to faith in the Messiah? Were they expected to honor the Sabbath? In Acts 15, when the leaders in Jerusalem were trying to figure out what to do about the influx of Gentile believers in Yeshua, James, the presiding officer of the Jerusalem council, decreed that the Gentiles must follow four basic rules:

> Therefore my judgment is that we should not trouble those
> of the Gentiles who turn to God, but should write to them
> to abstain from the things polluted by idols, and from sexual
> immorality, and from what has been strangled, and from
> blood.
> —Acts 15:19-20

These four rules were obviously not intended to be the full expression of Gentile obedience since they don't even begin to address a number of extremely important moral issues. Rather, these four rules were the starting point for new Gentile believers to be received into the community and permitted to attend the synagogue meetings without

---

53   Justo L. González, *A Brief History of Sunday: From the New Testament to the New Creation* (Grand Rapids, MI: Wm. B. Eerdmans Publishing Co., 2017), 18.

offending the Jewish attendees.[54] In fact, in the very next verse, James says something interesting: "For from ancient generations Moses has had in every city those who proclaim him, for he is read every Sabbath in the synagogues" (Acts 15:21). This statement implies an expectation that the Gentiles would take part in the synagogue services every Sabbath to be instructed in Moses's teaching. The rules given in the preceding verse served as a starting point for the new believers; they would learn the rest of what God expected of them over time as they faithfully attended the meetings every Sabbath. Since the local synagogue was the only place where the Scriptures would even be accessible for the vast majority of people, this expectation makes complete sense in light of the Gentile believers' need to be trained in God's word. As J.K. McKee explains:

> The implication made by James is that once the new, non-Jewish Believers abstained from idols, sexual immorality, strangled meats, and blood, they would really be able to go to the synagogues to hear the Torah of Moses taught. Many of them were already doing this, but the degree to which they were able to fellowship with Jewish Believers was being hampered, perhaps because no clear guidelines for table fellowship had been agreed upon. They needed to be welcomed into the assembly, and Jewish Believers needed to help and mentor them in their new walk of faith, guided by the grace of Messiah Yeshua which had saved them both. (Likewise, if the non-Jews started to follow some clear, beginner's guidelines, any Jewish non-Be-

---

54   Acts 15 is covered in greater detail in chapter 4.

THE NEW TESTAMENT CASE FOR SABBATH OBSERVANCE

lievers might be able to recognize that these Believers in Israel's Messiah were not quite so "pagan" after all.)[55]

What other evidence supports the idea that early Christians were committed to honoring the Sabbath? Acts 21 is a key passage that speaks to this. Thirty years after Yeshua commanded his disciples to proclaim the gospel and make disciples of all nations (Matthew 28:19-20), James informs Paul of "how many thousands there are among the Jews of those who have believed" (Acts 21:20). In Greek, "thousands" is literally "tens of thousands." According to Craig Keener, "Given current estimates of Jerusalem's population in this period at perhaps eighty thousand, and that most Judeans were rural, the literal figure is not impossible."[56] But even if Luke uses this term hyperbolically, "it is unlikely that he would have merely invented a massive Jerusalem church."[57] This point is significant since James describes this large number of Jewish Christians as "all zealous for the law" (Acts 21:20), which means they kept the Sabbath and considered it a very important aspect of their faith in Yeshua. This fact is not what we would expect if Yeshua and the apostles taught that the Sabbath was no longer necessary.

What is even more striking about this passage is what it teaches us about Paul's theology. Apparently, there was some confusion regarding Paul's teachings. Some of the Jerusalem believers heard rumors that Paul taught the Jewish Christians to "forsake Moses" (Torah) and not circumcise their children (Acts 20:21). James knew that these rumors

---

55   J.K. McKee, *The New Testament Validates Torah* (Richardson, TX: Messianic Apologetics, 2012), 86.

56   Craig Keener, *Acts* (Cambridge University Press, 2020), 517.

57   Ibid.

28   DAVID WILBER

were false, so he admonished Paul to participate in a purification ritual at the temple precincts in order to reassure the Jerusalem Christians publicly that the rumors about him were baseless and that Paul himself lived "in observance of the law" (Acts 20:22-24). And that is what Paul did (Acts 21:26). Paul's actions in this passage are not what we would expect if he taught against the Torah, but his actions *are* what we would expect if he upheld the Torah (and by extension the Sabbath) as an important aspect of one's faith in Yeshua.[58]

In summary, by their faithful observance, both the words and behavior of Yeshua and the apostles testify to the Sabbath's ongoing relevance. The suggestion that the apostles regularly attended Sabbath services as a mere missionary strategy assumes too much. A natural reading of the relevant texts reveals what we would expect from faithful Jews: they kept the Sabbath. Additionally, they not only kept the

---

58   Some might argue that the inclusion of the Jerusalem Council's ruling in Acts 21:25 is a contrasting remark to Acts 21:23-24. That is, while Paul needs to demonstrate his full Torah observance, Gentiles do not need to go beyond the four rules given in Acts 21:25 (cf. Acts 15:20). But as I have mentioned previously, the four rules were obviously not intended to be the full expression of Gentile obedience. Rather, these four rules were the starting point for new Gentile believers to be received into the community and permitted to attend the synagogue meetings without offending the Jewish attendees. J.K. McKee offers a reasonable explanation for the reiteration of the decree in Acts 21:25: "The placement of v. 25 within James' and the Jerusalem leaders' discussion with Paul does not at all need to be taken as meaning that the non-Jewish Believers were not required to progress beyond the four prohibitions...Vs. 22-25 are used to remind the reader that the Apostle Paul is a man who is 'orderly, keeping the Law' because 'concerning the Gentiles who have believed, we wrote...,' which Paul at the Jerusalem Council agreed to. Paul's implementation of the Apostolic decree among the nations confirms his obedience to the Torah, that he is not rogue and completely independent from Jerusalem, and that the introduction of non-Jews is not tantamount to introducing Greco-Roman paganism into the *ekklesia!*" (J.K. McKee, *Acts 15 For The Practical Messianic* [McKinney, TX: Messianic Apologetics, 2010], 192.)

Sabbath themselves but also expected new Gentile converts to attend Sabbath services alongside Jewish believers regularly. Finally, thirty years after Yeshua's earthly ministry, we see that "thousands" of Jerusalem Christians were still zealous for the Torah and still observing the Sabbath. Paul went to some length to reassure these Christians that the rumors about him were false and that he also lived in accordance with the Torah, which is what we would expect from someone who affirmed the ongoing validity of the Sabbath.

Additional New Testament Texts Supporting Sabbath Observance

What did Paul have to say about the Sabbath? Like Yeshua, Paul also affirmed the Torah's enduring validity. We see this clearly in the book of Romans. Paul declares that our faith does not overthrow the Torah, but rather establishes it (Romans 3:31). He teaches that sin is defined as breaking the Torah's commandments (Romans 7:7) and admonishes believers not to continue living in sin (Romans 6:1-2). He calls the Torah holy, righteous, and good (Romans 7:12). He calls the Torah spiritual (Romans 7:14) and says he delights in it (Romans 7:22). He says the Holy Spirit empowers believers to keep the Torah (Romans 8:2-4). Why is this important? Because the command to keep the Sabbath is part of the Torah. Thus, by upholding the Torah's validity, Paul upholds the Sabbath's validity.

Additionally, in his second letter to Timothy, Paul declared, "All Scripture is breathed out by God and profitable for teaching, for reproof, for correction, and for training in righteousness, that the man of God may be complete, equipped for every good work" (2 Timothy 3:16-17). The "Scripture" to which Paul refers is what Timothy was acquainted with from childhood (2 Timothy 3:15). Specifically, Scripture here refers "to what we know as the Old Testament and what the Jewish people call the *Tanach*."[59] Thus, all Scripture, and the Old Testament in particular, is profitable for "teaching, for reproof, for correction, and for training in righteousness." This statement from Paul implicitly affirms the Sabbath commandment as God-breathed and profitable to Christians since it is included in "all Scripture."

Do any other apostles support this position? Yes! The apostle Peter also implies that Christians should keep the Sabbath. In his first epistle he writes, "As obedient children, do not be conformed to the passions of your former ignorance, but as he who called you is holy, you also be holy in all your conduct, since it is written, 'You shall be holy, for I am holy'" (1 Peter 1:14-16). Our salvation experience through Yeshua's work leads to a life of holiness. That is the biblical pattern: God grants salvation and then calls his people into faithful service for his glory. It was the same pattern with Israel: God saved them out of Egypt and then gave them the Torah so they could serve him and be an example to the nations (Deuteronomy 4:5-8). God's gift of salvation comes with the responsibility on our part to love God and serve him, to be holy.

However, Peter's admonition raises a question: what exactly does holiness look like? How do we "be holy" in all our conduct? Peter tells us where to look to find out—he says, "it is written." So, if we want to know what Peter meant when he called us to be holy, we have to look at where it is written! God's command to be holy as he is holy occurs a few times in the book of Leviticus (Leviticus 11:44; 19:2; 20:7, 26). The context of these passages concerns various laws regarding how God's people are to live. For instance, Leviticus 19:2 says, "You shall be holy, for I the LORD your God am holy," and then the rest of the chapter defines holy conduct. Among various other laws, "you shall keep my Sabbaths" (Leviticus 19:3) is defined as holy conduct.

---

59   Walter L. Liefeld, *1 & 2 Timothy, Titus* (Grand Rapids, MI: Zondervan, 1999), 279.

The apostle John also has some relevant remarks on this topic. John constantly reminds his readers of the importance of keeping God's commandments. He says that those who have truly come to know the Messiah will keep his commandments (1 John 2:3-4) and that our keeping of God's commandments is how we know we love God and our neighbor (1 John 5:2-3). Do the commandments John refers to include the Sabbath? That seems likely when we read 1 John in context. For instance, after he says that those who know the Messiah will keep his commandments in 1 John 2:3-4, he says that those who abide in Messiah "ought to walk in the same way in which he walked" (1 John 2:6). Considering Yeshua's own faithful Sabbath observance and his teaching in Matthew 5:17-20, it seems reasonable that John's admonition to keep God's commandments would include the command to keep the Sabbath.

Additionally, James writes that Christians are to be "doers of the word" (James 1:22). What word? The Torah! As Scot McKnight observes, "Torah and 'do' (*'asah*) are brought together so often in the Hebrew Bible that instinct ought to lead us to see here a form of Torah observance."[60] This fact is made clear a couple of verses later when James speaks of being a doer of the "perfect law, the law of liberty," which is an obvious reference to the Torah.[61] For James, the Torah is

---

60   Scot McKnight, *The New International Commentary of the New Testament: The Letter of James* (Grand Rapids, MI: Wm. B. Eerdmans Publishing Co., 2011) p. 147.

61   See Tim Hegg, *A Commentary on the Epistle of James* (Tacoma, WA: TorahResource, 2021), 58, 60-61: "Clearly James' description of the "law" as both perfect and liberating makes it clear that he is talking about the Torah, the very Law of God given to Moses and proclaimed to Israel...Note carefully that the 'law' to which James refers is the very word of God, all of it, including and even based upon the Torah which Moses brought down from Sinai and the subsequent revelations given to Moses by God Himself. Far from replacing the Torah with the later Apostolic Scriptures as some teach, James is clearly establishing for us the utter necessity of the Torah and that it is the very foundation upon

perfect and brings liberty, echoing the same attitude toward the Torah we see expressed in the Psalms, particularly Psalm 19:7-11.[62] And from James's perspective, the "word" (Torah) that we are to be doers of includes the Sabbath.

Finally, the author of Hebrews also indicates that Sabbath observance is still expected of Christians. He says, "there remains a Sabbath rest for the people of God" (Hebrews 4:9). Some have suggested that Hebrews 3:7-4:11 implies that the Sabbath was replaced with a spiritualized version of the commandment and that Christians now "keep" the Sabbath by "resting in Christ."[63] However, the word for "Sabbath rest" in this verse is *sabbatismos*, which refers to the literal act of resting on the Sabbath day.[64] According to A. T. Lincoln, "the term denotes the observance or celebration of the Sabbath." Lincoln further notes that *sabbatismos* "corresponds to the Septuagint usage of the cognate verb

---

which the believer's life of liberty is founded."

62 See Ibid, 58-59: "[I]t seems very likely that James has Ps 19 in his mind as he, being carried along by the Ruach HaKodesh, wrote these words. For in Ps 19:7[8] we read: 'The law of the LORD is perfect, restoring the soul; the testimony of the LORD is sure, making wise the simple (Ps 19:7 [Hebrew v. 8]).' Granted, the LXX of this verse in Ps 19 does not use the same word for "perfect" (*teleios*) as we find in our James text. But the fact that the Greek word [*nomos*] is regularly used to translate the Hebrew [*torah*] in the LXX (89% of the times) would give strong support to the fact that James refers to the Torah of Moses (the first five books of the Tanach) when he speaks of "the perfect law." Note also that Ps 19:7[8] has [*ho nomos tou kuriou amōmos*] in the LXX, once again translating [*torah*] with the Greek *nomos*."

63 I address this objection to literal Sabbath observance in chapter 2.

64 See Samuele Bacchiocchi, *The Sabbath in the New Testament* (Berrien Springs, MI: Biblical Perspectives, 2000), 50: "[*sabbatismos*] is used several times as a technical term for Sabbathkeeping in post-canonical literature by Plutarch, Justin, Epiphanius, the Apostolic Constitutions and the Martyrdom of Peter and Paul." Bacchiocchi references Plutarch, *De Superstitione* 3 (Moralia 1660); Justin Martyr, *Dialogue with Trypho* 23, 3; Epiphanius, *Adversus Haereses* 30, 2, 2; *Apostolic Constitutions* 2, 36.

sabbatizo (cf. Ex 16:23; Lev 23:32; 26:34f; 2 Chron 36:21), which also has reference to Sabbath observance."[65] Thus, the author of Hebrews explicitly states that literal Sabbath rest (observance) "remains" for the people of God.

In summary, Paul, Peter, John, James, and the author of Hebrews each affirm the Sabbath's continuing validity. The Sabbath is part of the Torah that Paul says the Holy Spirit empowers us to keep. Peter says that Christians must be holy in all our conduct, and keeping the Sabbath is part of what defines holy conduct. John says that genuine Christians will keep God's commandments, which undoubtedly includes the commandment to keep the Sabbath. James says that Christians must be "doers of the word," which implies Sabbath observance. Finally, the author of Hebrews indicates that Sabbath observance is still relevant to God's people.

Conclusion

In this chapter, we saw that Yeshua affirmed the Sabbath's enduring validity as part of the Torah in Matthew 5:17-20. In Mark 2:27, we saw that Yeshua expressed the Sabbath's universal and perpetual nature when he said that the Sabbath was established in creation for all mankind. In the book of Acts, we learned that the apostles observed the Sabbath and expected even new Gentile converts to observe it too. Finally, when we examined writings from Paul, Peter, John, James, and Hebrews, we saw that they contained instructions indicating that the Sabbath is still relevant to Christians. Based on these passages from the New Testament, it is clear that Christians should observe the Sabbath.

---

65   A.T. Lincoln, "Sabbath, Rest, and Eschatology in the New Testament," *From Sabbath to Lord's Day: A Biblical, Historical, and Theological Investigation* (Grand Rapids, MI: Zondervan, 1982), 213.

CHAPTER 2

ANSWERING OBJECTIONS: THE SABBATH WAS REPEALED

It is a commonly held belief within Christian circles that the Sabbath is no longer important. This belief is based on a few passages from the New Testament—namely, Matthew 12:1-8 (cf. Mark 2:23-28; Luke 6:1-5), Colossians 2:16-17, Romans 14:5, Galatians 4:8-11, and Hebrews 3:7-4:11. In the previous chapter, I made the case that the New Testament agrees with the Old Testament about the Sabbath— that God's people should still observe the Sabbath. If that is true, then how can there be New Testament passages that declare the Sabbath to be optional, or even void? This chapter will reconcile this apparent contradiction and demonstrate that all Scripture is consistent in proclaiming the Sabbath's ongoing validity.

Matthew 12:1-8 (Mark 2:23-28; Luke 6:1-5) — Lord of the Sabbath

The synoptic gospels record a story that is frequently interpreted to be an example of Yeshua violating and teaching against the Sabbath. The narrative begins with Yeshua and his disciples walking through the grainfields on the Sabbath and the disciples plucking heads of grain to eat (Matthew 12:1; Mark 2:23; Luke 6:1). The Pharisees confront Yeshua and his disciples and accuse them of violating the Sabbath (Matthew 12:2; Mark 2:24; Luke 6:2). Yeshua defends his disciples, giving the example of David entering the house of God and eating the bread of the Presence, which was meant only for the priests (Matthew

12:3-4; Mark 2:25-26; Luke 6:3-4). Matthew includes Yeshua's additional examples of the priests being guiltless even though they work in the temple on the Sabbath (Matthew 12:5) and Yeshua's statement that "something greater than the temple is here" (Matthew 12:6). Matthew also includes Yeshua admonishing the Pharisees that they would not have condemned the guiltless if they knew what it meant when Scripture says, "I desire mercy, and not sacrifice" (Matthew 12:7). Mark includes Yeshua's additional statement that the Sabbath was made for man, not man for the Sabbath (Mark 2:27). Finally, Yeshua declares that he, the Son of Man, is lord of the Sabbath (Matthew 12:8; Mark 2:28; Luke 6:5).

Once again, a popular interpretation of these texts is that Yeshua justifies his disciples' transgression of the Sabbath by declaring his lordship over the Sabbath. Additionally, some even argue that this incident demonstrates Yeshua's intention to abolish the Sabbath entirely. While commenting on these passages, Christian pastor and theologian John MacArthur says this:

> Jesus, rather than acquiescing to their concern over a violation of the Sabbath, points to other violations of the Sabbath. In verse 8 [of Matthew 12], He says, "The Son of Man is Lord of the Sabbath." He can do anything He wants with the Sabbath. He can institute it. He can make commands for restrictions. He can require death for violation of those commands, as in the Mosaic law. Or He can set it aside, totally. He can abrogate it. He can nullify it. And there is the transition that is taking place in the New Testament … Jesus is announcing the end of the Sabbath.[1]

---

1   John MacArthur, "Understanding the Sabbath," *Grace to You*. www.gty.org.

Does this incident in the gospels really suggest that Yeshua announced the end of the Sabbath? That interpretation is unlikely for several reasons.

First, as we discussed in chapter 1, Yeshua upheld the Sabbath commandment by unequivocally affirming the Torah in Matthew 5:17-20. He said not a single iota or dot would pass away from the Torah until the end of the age and the consummation of the kingdom, when heaven and earth pass away (Matthew 5:18; cf. Revelation 21:1ff). He also admonished his followers to do and teach even the least of the Torah's commandments (Matthew 5:19). Yeshua made this statement only a few chapters before this confrontation with the Pharisees recorded in Matthew 12. Why would he announce the end of the Sabbath commandment shortly after he affirmed its enduring validity?

Second, since sin is transgression of the Torah by definition (Romans 7:7; 1 John 3:4), breaking the Sabbath is considered sin. Yet, Scripture teaches that Yeshua was without sin (Hebrews 4:15; 1 Peter 1:22). Thus, Yeshua being "lord of the Sabbath" surely can't mean that he freely violated the Sabbath since that would make him a sinner.

Third, Scripture defines a false prophet as one who tries to turn God's people away from doing what God commanded them (Deuteronomy 13:5). Since God commanded his people to observe the Sabbath day, anyone who comes as a prophet and announces the end of the Sabbath is a false prophet by definition. Since Yeshua is not a false prophet, he can't have endorsed the violation or abandonment of the Sabbath.

With all of that considered, let's take a closer look to see what is actually going on in these passages.

> At that time Jesus went through the grainfields on the Sabbath.
> His disciples were hungry, and they began to pluck heads of

> grain and to eat. But when the Pharisees saw it, they said to
> him, "Look, your disciples are doing what is not lawful to do
> on the Sabbath." —Matthew 12:1-3 (cf. Mark 2:23-24; Luke
> 6:1-2)

The first thing to note is that the controversy was not that the
disciples were plucking heads of grain, which the Torah permitted
(Deuteronomy 23:25). The problem, in the minds of the Pharisees,
was that the disciples were plucking heads of grain *on the Sabbath*. But
why was this an issue? Do the Sabbath laws in the Torah prohibit such
an activity? No. Nowhere does the Torah prohibit plucking heads of
grain on the Sabbath.

When we look at what the Torah *does* say about the Sabbath, we see
that regular work was forbidden (Exodus 20:8-11), and this included
harvesting (Exodus 34:21). Apparently, the Pharisees considered the
disciples' activity a type of harvesting. In the rabbinic literature, particularly the Mishnah, there are thirty-nine classifications of prohibited
"work" on the Sabbath (m.*Shabbat* 7.2). One of these prohibited activ-
ities is "reaping." According to Matthew Thiessen, "The rabbis flesh
out what this category of work entails in the Tosefta—it includes the
plucking of grain as a subset of reaping"[2] (Tosefta, *Shabbat* 9.17). Based
on the Pharisees' accusations, it seems likely that this Sabbath restriction was already in force in the first century. Thus, from the Pharisees'
perspective, the disciples' act of plucking heads of grain constituted a
violation of the Sabbath.

However, the disciples' activity was a violation of only man-made
restrictions, not the Torah. In fact, in the Torah itself, plucking heads

---

2   Matthew Thiessen, *Jesus and the Forces of Death: The Gospels' Portrayal of Ritual Impurity Within First-Century Judaism* (Grand Rapids, MI: BakerAcademic, 2020), 156.

of grain is *a distinct activity* from harvesting: "If you go into your neighbor's standing grain, you may pluck the ears with your hand, but you shall not put a sickle to your neighbor's standing grain" (Deuteronomy 23:25).[3] The reason for this law in Deuteronomy was to foster a community of love and trust between neighbors. Owners of fields were not to be greedy with God's blessings produced from the land. Instead, they were to allow hungry passers-by to pick some of the grain or fruit from the fields for their personal needs. However, these travelers were not to be greedy either. They couldn't disrespect the owners of these fields by taking a sickle to the grain and harvesting large amounts of their neighbors' produce. That would be tantamount to stealing. As Jeffrey Tigay writes, "Since a sickle cuts several stalks at once, this could easily yield more than one can eat on the spot, which is all one is entitled to take."[4]

The Bible clearly indicates that harvesting involves gathering much more produce than what one would be able to eat on the spot (e.g., Leviticus 19:9-10). Thus, unlike the rabbinic rulings, the Torah itself indicates that harvesting, which involved taking a sickle to the grain (Deuteronomy 16:9), *is something different* from merely plucking heads of grain with your hand. In light of this, the disciples were not "harvesting," and therefore, they were not violating the Sabbath according to the Torah. The Pharisees were condemning the disciples based on their own unreasonably strict man-made rules.

That Yeshua's disciples were, in fact, *not* violating the Sabbath makes sense in light of Yeshua's response to the Pharisees. As we con-

---

3   See Tim Hegg, *Why We Keep Torah: 10 Persistent Questions* (Tacoma, WA: TorahResource, 2009), 41: "Here, to 'wield a sickle' (=hervesting) is differentiated from plucking heads of grain. So while the Torah itself prohibits harvesting on the Sabbath, plucking heads of grain is not defined as harvesting and would therefore be allowed."

4   Jeffrey Tigay, *Deuteronomy* (Jerusalem: The Jewish Publican Society, 1996), 220.

tinue in the passage, we see that Yeshua defends his disciples against the Pharisees' accusation. He says his disciples are innocent of wrongdoing (Matthew 12:7). His argument is not that the Sabbath is no longer important. Instead, his argument is that the Pharisees' accusation is baseless and that his disciples did not violate the Sabbath at all. This defense is not what we would expect from someone announcing the end of the Sabbath, but it *is* what we would expect from someone who considered the Sabbath to be important.

Furthermore, it is no coincidence that this controversy immediately follows Yeshua's invitation in the previous chapter of Matthew to take his yoke of teaching upon oneself and to learn from him (Matthew 11:28-30). Yeshua's yoke is easy and his burden light. His yoke (that is, his teaching) provides real rest. This is in contrast to the heavy burden of the Pharisees' teaching (Matthew 23:4), and this confrontation with the Pharisees highlights that difference.

> He said to them, "Have you not read what David did when he was hungry, and those who were with him: how he entered the house of God and ate the bread of the Presence, which it was not lawful for him to eat nor for those who were with him, but only for the priests?
> —Matthew 12:3-4 (cf. Mark 2:25-26; Luke 6:3-4)

In defending his disciples, Yeshua appeals to when David and his men were weary from battle, and they entered the house of God and ate the bread of the Presence. This act violated the Torah since that bread was for the priests alone to eat (1 Samuel 21:1-6; Leviticus 24:9). Why would Yeshua answer the Pharisees' accusation in this way? What does David eating bread have to do with this conversation about the Sabbath? While David's act was a violation of the Torah, Yeshua understood that the Pharisees likely considered it to be justified in light of the situation. David and his men were in the midst of battle, and their lives may have depended upon acquiring the sacred bread from the high priest for food. Most Jewish teachers agreed that some laws of the Torah could be justifiably suspended based on the principle of *pikuach nefesh*, or "preservation of life" (b.Yoma 85a-b). Again, the Pharisees likely considered David's situation to have been a necessary exception to the laws governing the bread of the Presence. Preservation of life justifies the transgression of laws that should otherwise be kept. It appears that Yeshua himself agreed with this principle, as he uses it a few verses later to support his argument that it is lawful to do good on the Sabbath:

> He said to them, "Which one of you who has a sheep, if it falls into a pit on the Sabbath, will not take hold of it and lift it out? Of how much more value is a man than a sheep! So it is lawful to do good on the Sabbath."
> —Matthew 12:11-12)

When Yeshua mentioned David eating the bread of the Presence, he was highlighting the Pharisees' neglect of the Torah's "weightier matters," which is something he regularly criticized them for (e.g., Matthew 23:23). Yeshua wanted to demonstrate that even though Sabbath observance is important, mercy and kindness are more important. Matthew records that the disciples were "hungry" (Matthew 12:1), and human needs must be prioritized above other rules. This is especially the case if those other rules aren't clearly expressed in the Scriptures themselves, like these rabbinic rules against plucking grain. Thus, in their effort to safeguard the Sabbath, the Pharisees ended up condemning the innocent on the basis of their man-made restrictions that didn't emphasize human wellbeing. Yeshua's appeal to David also exposed the Pharisees' inconsistency and hypocrisy. The Pharisees understandably would have considered David's actions to be justified even though he violated the Torah. How much more should they have considered the disciples' actions justified, especially when all *they* violated were man-made rules?

Yeshua gives another example in defense of his disciples' actions:

> Or have you not read in the Law how on the Sabbath the priests in the temple profane the Sabbath and are guiltless? I tell you, something greater than the temple is here.
> —Matthew 12:5-6

The priests were required to do some work on the Sabbath, such as administering the Sabbath sacrifices (e.g., Numbers 28:9-10), and yet they are considered innocent. However, nowhere does the Torah indicate that it is a violation of the Sabbath for priests to perform their duties. The Pharisees likely reasoned that the laws of the sacrificial system supersede *their laws* pertaining to the Sabbath (b.*Shabbat* 132b), and thus Yeshua simply applied that same line of logic in his response to them. According to the Pharisees, the requirements of the temple service are of greater importance than the Pharisees' rules regarding the Sabbath. In light of this fact, the priests are justified in breaking the Pharisees' Sabbath rules when they perform their temple service. Moreover, Yeshua is greater than the temple. Therefore, Yeshua's disciples are also justified in disregarding the Pharisees' rules regarding the Sabbath.

Remember, this confrontation is about whether or not Yeshua's disciples violated the Sabbath. Yeshua wants to demonstrate that the Pharisees have unjustly condemned his disciples, who are "guiltless" (Matthew 12:7). If the Pharisees were willing to consider the priests innocent of transgressing the Sabbath, since Yeshua is greater than the temple, how much more should they have considered Yeshua's disciples innocent?

> And if you had known what this means, 'I desire mercy, and
> not sacrifice,' you would not have condemned the guiltless.
> —Matthew 12:7

Here Yeshua quotes Hosea and says that if the Pharisees had understood Hosea's message, they would not have condemned his disciples. What is that message? That mercy or compassion must take precedence when it comes to Torah observance. Again, the issue seems to be the Pharisees' neglect of the Torah's "weightier matters." The Pharisees were so fixated on safeguarding the Sabbath by adding a bunch of man-made restrictions that they abandoned the greater principles of the Torah, namely compassion. The irony of this is that the Pharisees' approach distorted the very purpose that God intended for the Sabbath from the beginning.

This is ultimately Yeshua's point: the Pharisees, through their misplaced priorities and excessive regulations, had turned the Sabbath into a meaningless and burdensome ritual. This is not what God desires. The Sabbath is intended to be a day of joy and rest (Exodus 23:12; Isaiah 58:13). It was a day to express one's love not only toward God but also toward one's neighbor. The Sabbath is to be enjoyed as a gift from God, observed with heartfelt gratitude. If the Pharisees understood this, they would not have condemned Yeshua's disciples.

Once again, Yeshua gives these examples to prove that his disciples are innocent of any Sabbath violation. If Yeshua meant for these examples to support some supposed right to disregard the Sabbath, he would not have said his disciples were guiltless. Rather, we would expect him to perhaps agree with the Pharisees and say something like, "Yes, my disciples are guilty of breaking the Sabbath, but it doesn't matter because the Sabbath isn't important anymore now that I'm here." But he doesn't say anything like that. Instead, he goes to some length to show that his disciples did *not* violate the Sabbath and that the Pharisees' way of keeping the Sabbath was not what God intended. Yeshua does not disregard the Sabbath, only the Pharisees' improper interpretation of it. The quotation from Hosea is meant to indicate that the Pharisees failed to understand what God really desires with regard to the Sabbath. As J. Andrew Overman writes:

> Matthew stresses that the disciples of Jesus are guiltless and have not violated the law. The problem is that the Pharisees do not understand the law properly. This is made explicit by the application of Hos. 6:6 in this context by Matthew. Jesus and his disciples do not break the law. **They break with the Pharisees over interpretation of the law, but not with regard to its validity or importance**. The law and its application, in Matthew's view, are to be understood primarily in terms of Jesus' demand for compassion. It is this "core value" that guides the application of the Sabbath laws. [Emphasis added][5]

God did not intend the Sabbath as a day to scold others for not conforming to man-made rules. God desires the Sabbath to be a day for joy and healing and mercy. The Sabbath is a day to show compassion and do good, as clearly demonstrated a little later with the story of Yeshua healing the man's hand on the Sabbath (Mark 12:9-13; Mark

---

5   J. Andrew Overman, *Matthew's Gospel and Formative Judaism: The Social World of the Matthean Community* (Minneapolis: Fortress Press, 1990), 81.

3:1-5; Luke 6:6-10). And that brings us to another statement from Yeshua, which is found in Mark's account of this incident:

> And he said to them, "The Sabbath was made for man, not
> man for the Sabbath."
> —Mark 2:27

Yeshua's point here is that God made the Sabbath to benefit humanity. This approach counters the Pharisaic approach to the Sabbath, which had turned the day into a burden through unreasonable man-made rules and a disregard for important principles like mercy. Moreover, as we covered in chapter 1, this statement implies the Sabbath's universal and perpetual nature. God made the Sabbath in the beginning to bless humanity. Thus, far from abolishing the Sabbath, in this verse, Yeshua teaches that the Sabbath is part of the creative order; it was established from creation as a gift intended to benefit all of mankind forever. That brings us to Yeshua's final statement in this conformation:

> For the Son of Man is lord of the Sabbath.
> —Matthew 12:8 (cf. Mark 2:28; Luke 6:5)

Yeshua's concluding remark in this exchange with the Pharisees is to announce that he is lord of the Sabbath. Was Yeshua declaring that he had the authority to nullify the Sabbath? As we have seen, that understanding does not align with Yeshua's overall argument. Yeshua defends his disciples and says they are innocent of the Pharisees' charges. If he were making the argument that he and his disciples had the right to disregard the Sabbath, he would have simply said so. Instead, he denies the Pharisees' accusation. A better understanding is that Yeshua declares himself to be the lord—the ultimate authority—regarding *how to interpret* the Sabbath. He, not the Pharisees, has the authority to determine what it means to keep the Sabbath properly.

This interpretation fits the overall theme we have examined, and it can be traced through all of Yeshua's conflicts with the religious leaders of his day. The gospels present Yeshua as the supreme interpreter of the Torah. Yeshua possesses the definitive interpretation and true meaning of the Torah, in contrast to the teachings of the scribes and Pharisees. We see this clearly in the Sermon on the Mount. Yeshua fulfills the Torah—that is, brings it to its intended meaning and application (Matthew 5:17). Contrary to the Pharisees' shallow or outright erroneous interpretations of the Torah, Yeshua explains what it really means to keep the Torah's commands. He teaches that one's righteousness must surpass that of the scribes and Pharisees (Matthew 5:20), and then goes on to explain what that means by expounding on various Torah laws, contrasting his teaching with theirs.

Consider the very end of Yeshua's Sermon on the Mount. When he finishes his teaching, the people were amazed and already beginning to recognize his authority:

> And when Jesus finished these sayings, the crowds were astonished at his teaching, for he was teaching them as one who had authority, and not as their scribes.
> —Matthew 7:28-29

Yeshua was not just another religious teacher like the scribes and Pharisees. He didn't just give his opinion. Yeshua's teaching on the Torah carried divine authority—an authority the Pharisees lacked. The Pharisees' teachings were merely words of men, whereas Yeshua's teachings were the words of God. When Yeshua taught, he spoke as "the fulfillment *par excellence* of the prophet spoken of by Moses,"[6] whose words were God's own words (Deuteronomy 18:18). Yeshua's possession of this divine authority does not indicate that he disregards the authority of the Torah. Rather, he establishes the Torah and, because of his own authority, he is able to clarify its true meaning and application.

This theme is evident in the confrontation with the Pharisees in Matthew 12, Mark 2, and Luke 6. In contrast to the Pharisees' improper interpretations of the Sabbath, Yeshua explains the purpose of the Sabbath and what it really means to keep it in accordance with God's will. He explains that his disciples are not guilty of breaking the Sabbath; they violated only the Pharisees' misguided *interpretation* of the Sabbath laws. Then, Yeshua concludes his answer to the Pharisees by asserting his authority explicitly: he, the Son of Man, is lord of the Sabbath. The title, "Son of Man," brings to mind Daniel's prophecy, where one like a son of man is seated alongside the Ancient of Days and given full authority and power over all creation (Daniel 7:13-14). Later in Matthew, we see that Yeshua's resurrection settled indisputably the reality of his ultimate authority for all to see. Just prior to his ascension, Yeshua declares, "All authority in heaven and on earth has been given to me" (Matthew 28:18). This authority includes giving the definitive interpretation of the Sabbath laws. As I. Howard Marshall writes, "surely the point of the saying is that here Jesus claims an authority tantamount to that of God with respect to the interpretation of the law."[7]

In summary, the Pharisees dared to accuse Yeshua's disciples of transgressing the Sabbath based on the Pharisees' own misplaced priorities and added man-made restrictions that had turned the Sab-

6   Tim Hegg, *The Gospel of Matthew: Chapters 1-7* (Tacoma: TorahResource, 2007), 282.
7   I. Howard Marshall, *Luke* (Grand Rapids, MI: Wm. B. Eerdmans Publishing, 1978), 233.

bath into a burdensome yoke. Yeshua defended his disciples, said they were innocent, and asserted his authority as the rightful interpreter of the commandment. Far from nullifying the Sabbath, these passages demonstrate that Yeshua affirms the Sabbath's validity.

Colossians 2:16-17 — A Shadow of Things to Come

In Colossians 2:16-17, Paul refers to things like the Sabbath and festivals as shadows that point to Christ:

> Therefore let no one pass judgment on you in questions of food and drink, or with regard to a festival or a new moon or a Sabbath. These are a shadow of the things to come, but the substance belongs to Christ.
> —Colossians 2:16-17

Based on these verses, now that Christ—the substance—has come, are the shadows no longer of any importance? Were those commandments set aside and nailed to the cross (Colossians 2:14)? Some say yes. John MacArthur's comments are representative of this understanding:

> Don't let anybody hold you to a Sabbath. And that's referring to the weekly Sabbath, because the other festival Sabbaths are covered under the term "festival and new moon." Don't let anybody hold you to the Sabbath. It was part of the system that included the temple, the priesthood, the sacrifices. It's gone. It was only the shadow, not the substance ... Paul is saying, you no longer need the shadow, you have the substance.[8]

---

8   John MacArthur, "Understanding the Sabbath," *Grace to You*. www.gty.org.

Does Paul really declare that commandments like the Sabbath and festivals are irrelevant now that the Messiah has come? That is unlikely for a couple of reasons.

First, as we discussed in chapter 1, such an interpretation doesn't fit with the broader biblical witness of Paul's perspective on these commandments. For instance, throughout the New Testament, we see that Paul regularly attended and participated in the synagogue services on the Sabbath (Acts 13:14, 44; 16:13; 17:2; 18:4). Moreover, in Acts 20:16, we see Paul expressing an urgent desire to be in Jerusalem for the Feast of Shavuot (Pentecost). In 1 Corinthians 5:7-8, Paul instructs his readers on how they are to observe Passover. Based on Paul's behavior and teaching elsewhere in Scripture, it is difficult to imagine him thinking that these parts of the Torah became irrelevant in light of the Messiah's coming. Instead, these examples of Paul observing and teaching these commandments are what we would expect if he believed they were still important. Paul's life and testimony demonstrated his devotion to the Torah's holy days.

Second, the false teaching Paul addresses in Colossians is characterized as "according to human tradition" (Colossians 2:8). It is "according to human precepts and teachings" (Colossians 2:22). That description does not seem to apply to things like the Sabbath. Sabbaths and festivals were not human teachings; they were commanded by God.

Third, this false teaching is characterized further as being "not according to Christ" (Colossians 2:8). But we know that Christ affirmed every iota and dot of the Torah as having enduring authority in the lives of his followers (Matthew 5:18). He said his followers are to do and teach the Torah's commandments, which include the Sabbath and festivals (Matthew 5:19).

When we consider Paul's record of observing the biblical Sabbath and festivals, along with the fact that in Colossians 2 he is coming against what he calls "human teachings," it seems strange that he would discourage Sabbath, festival, and dietary law observance in Colossians 2:16-17. But aside from simply doubting the traditional interpretation of these verses, do we have any good reasons for accepting an alternative interpretation? Indeed, we do! When we examine the "Colossian heresy" in more detail, we learn that Paul was not opposed to commandments like the Sabbath *per se*. Instead, Paul opposed a *misuse* of these commandments. In the same way that Yeshua opposed the misuse of the commandments in Matthew 12, as a disciple of Yeshua, Paul was following in his master's footsteps.

Let's look at Colossians 2:8, which gives a description of the Colossian heresy:

> See to it that no one takes you captive by philosophy and empty deceit, according to human tradition, according to the elemental spirits of the world, and not according to Christ.
> —Colossians 2:8

The false doctrine influencing believers at Colossae is characterized first as "philosophy and empty deceit." The Greek term translated "philosophy" (*philosophia*) generally carries the sense of "manner of life" and often addresses ethics. For instance, Josephus describes the Essenes, Sadducees, and Pharisees as different "sects of philosophy" (*Antiq.* 18.11). In the Hellenistic Jewish literature, the word takes on what the scholar Nijay Gupta calls "a moralistic edge." Gupta writes:

A number of texts presume that a good and true philosophy has the ability to restrain sin and control wanton passions and desires.[9]

Gupta cites three historical sources that demonstrate this idea. For instance, in 4 Maccabees, written in the first or second century AD, Antiochus pressures the Jews to eat unclean foods. Eleazar defends the dietary laws of the Torah, as well as Judaism more broadly, calling it "our philosophy":

> You scoff at our philosophy as though living by it were irrational, but it teaches us self-control, so that we master all pleasures and desires, and it also trains us in courage, so that we endure any suffering willingly.
> —4 Maccabees 5:22-23, RSV

According to the *Letter of Aristeas*, written in the third or second century BC, Ptolmey asks the question, "What is philosophy?" A Jewish sage responds to Ptolmey with the following:

> To deliberate well in reference to any question that emerges... and never to be carried away by impulses, but to ponder over the injuries that result from the passions, and to act rightly as the circumstances demand, practicing moderation."[10]

Philo, a first-century Jewish philosopher, also has some relevant remarks: "Philosophy teaches temperance with regard to the belly, and

---

9   Nijay K. Gupta, *Colossians* (Macon, GA: Smyth and Helwys, 2013), 90.
10   Letter of Aristeas. Quoted in Gupta, *Colossians*, 90-91.

temperance with regard to the parts below the belly, and also temperance and restraint of the tongue."[11] These historical sources give us an idea of what Paul means by the word philosophy. Broadly speaking, it is a manner of life intended to develop self-control. The doctrine influencing the Colossian believers could be considered a type of philosophy, but according to Paul it is "empty deceit." It doesn't deliver what it promises. Paul says it is "of no value in stopping the indulgence of the flesh" (Colossians 2:23).

Another problem with this false teaching is that it is "according to human tradition." From Paul's perspective, mere human teachings are useless in overcoming the power of sin (Colossians 2:22-23).

Finally, this false teaching is according to "the elemental spirits of the world," which likely refers to spiritual beings that were believed to have control over nature and the cosmos. Philo writes about nations that made divinities out of the four elements of earth, water, air, and fire (*Decalogue* 53). The Wisdom of Solomon, a book written in the first century BC, speaks similarly about ignorant people who believe that the elements, such as wind, fire, water, etc., were gods who ruled the world (Wisdom of Solomon 13:1-2). Passages from the pseudepigrapha and Dead Sea Scrolls give some evidence of these types of ideas floating around broader Judaism of the Second Temple era.[12]

It appears that the false teachers at Colossae were enamored with cosmic authorities, supernatural powers over nature, and angels (Colossians 2:8, 15, 18, 20). They exalted and feared these spiritual entities, believing them to have control over the universe and their destinies. These superstitions were also combined with religious practices, including biblical holy days. In practice, this false philosophy strictly

---

11   Philo, *Congr. 80.* Quoted in Gupta, *Colossians,* 91.

12   1 Enoch 82:10-20; Jubilees 2:2; 1QM 10.11-12.

regulated foods, drinks, and festivals (2:16) and involved ascetic rituals and worship of angels (2:18-23). By adhering to the practices and regulations of these false teachers, people believed they could attain wisdom and be protected from the evil spirits that troubled them.

Hippolytus of Rome, a late second/early third century Christian theologian, wrote about the heretical teaching of a man named Elchasai (*A Refutation of All Heresies* 9.11). Elchasai's teaching gives us a fitting parallel to what we see happening at Colossae, where some teachers mixed elements of Judaism with astrological beliefs and practices. Citing Hippolytus, the scholar Clinton Arnold writes the following:

> There is one figure who may help us better understand how a Christian teacher may have combined magical, astrological, Jewish, and local pagan cult traditions into a new teaching. At the end of the first century, during the time of Trajan (A.D. 98-117), a Christian leader named Elchasai combined aspects of Jewish nomism (circumcision and law observance) with astrological beliefs and practices. The resultant syncretistic teaching emphasized the hostility of the stars (viewed as angels) and the need to regulate one's life according to the calendar (especially the Sabbath and the courses of the moon) … Colossae was certainly not afflicted by the teaching of Elchasai, but "the philosophy" bore many similarities. At the minimum, the example of Elchasai points to emerging forms of localized syncretistic Christianity at an early stage. The Elchasaite teaching also demonstrates how a magical/astrological interpretation of sabbaths could surface in early Christianity.[13]

---

13   Clinton E. Arnold, *The Colossian Syncretism: The Interface between Christianity and Folk Belief at Colossae* (Grand Rapids, MI: Baker Books, 1996), 217-218.

To give a summary of the false teaching at Colossae, it was a type of "philosophy"—that is, a manner of life intended to develop self-control. But according to Paul, it failed to deliver what it promised because it was according to mere human tradition and wrongly exalted elemental spirits and powers. This false teaching also incorporated the observance of some biblical practices mixed with ascetic rituals.

A big problem with this mystical false teaching is that it ultimately resulted in minimizing the Messiah's exalted position as the head from whom the body derives its life (Colossians 2:18-19). These false teachers worshiped angels and tried to appease the elemental spirits instead of looking to the Messiah. So, how does Paul counter this false teaching? He proclaims the preeminence of the Messiah:

- The Messiah is the real embodiment of wisdom and knowledge (Colossians 2:2-3).
- The Messiah is "the image of the invisible God" (Colossians 1:15). That is, God's full character is embodied in Messiah (cf. 2 Corinthians 4:4; Philippians 2:6; Hebrews 1:3).
- The Messiah is "the firstborn of all creation" (Colossians 1:15), which is an Old Testament title expressing royal status and authority (Psalm 89:27).
- It was by, through, and for Messiah that "all things were created, in heaven and on earth, visible and invisible, whether thrones or dominions or rulers or authorities" (Colossians 1:16). The invisible creations in heaven would include angelic beings. Paul's point is that the Messiah, the one by whom, through whom, and for whom all things were created, has authority and power over all created things in heaven and on earth.
- The Messiah is "before all things, and in him all things hold together" (Colossians 1:17). That is, the Messiah has priority in

terms of time and rank, and he is the sustainer of the universe (cf. Hebrews 1:3). Paul hopes to encourage the Colossian believers not to try to find coherence in the universe by turning to angels. The Messiah is the one who holds all things together.

- The Messiah is also "the head of the body, the church" (Colossians 1:18; 2:10, 18-19). That is, he is the lord over the church as well as its source of life: "...the Head, from whom the whole body, nourished and knit together through its joints and ligaments, grows with a growth that is from God" (Colossians 2:19).
- The Messiah is "the beginning, the firstborn from the dead, that in everything he might be preeminent" (Colossians 1:18). That is, the Messiah's resurrection has inaugurated the kingdom—his resurrection being the "firstfruits," assuring us of the full harvest to come at the end of the age (cf. 1 Corinthians 15:20, 23). In the meantime, the Messiah exercises his rule through his body, the church.
- The Messiah is one in whom "all the fullness of God was pleased to dwell" (Colossians 1:19; 2:9). As F.F. Bruce puts it, "all the attributes of God—his spirit, word, wisdom, and glory—are disclosed in him."[14]

Paul made this proclamation to set the record straight about who was really in charge. He wanted to warn the Colossian believers not to be led astray by mystical teachings involving things like angel worship. His concern was that these false teachings relegated the Messiah, who is head over all rule and authority in creation, to the theological background. Thus, Paul encouraged the Colossian believers to look to the Messiah alone to satisfy their yearning for spiritual fulfillment

---

14   F.F. Bruce, *Colossians, Philemon, Ephesians* (Grand Rapids, MI: Eerdmands, 1984), 74.

(Colossians 2:10). This is why he goes to some length to express the supremacy of the Messiah.

Paul makes one more significant point in his argument for the Messiah's preeminence. He proclaims that only the Messiah's work on the cross provides forgiveness of sin and reconciliation with God (Colossians 1:20; 2:11-14). Redemption cannot be found anywhere else, least of all through a strict observance of ascetic rituals to appease angelic powers. The Messiah's work also had the effect of defeating the spiritual rulers and authorities (Colossians 2:15).

To demonstrate his point about redemption and reconciliation, Paul uses the metaphors of circumcision, baptism, and the "record of debt" (Colossians 2:11-14). Paul's circumcision metaphor here expresses our dying in Messiah's death—that is, "putting off the body of the flesh." Paul then moves to baptism to express our being buried and rising in union with Messiah in his burial and resurrection. When we put our faith in the Messiah, we die with him, enter his tomb with him, and are raised with him. The third metaphor Paul uses, the "record of debt," has caused some confusion. Did Paul teach that the Messiah took away the Torah and nailed it to the cross?

> And you, who were dead in your trespasses and the uncircumcision of your flesh, God made alive together with him, having forgiven us all our trespasses, by canceling the record of debt that stood against us with its legal demands. This he set aside, nailing it to the cross.
> —Colossians 2:13-14

The interpretation that Messiah set aside the Torah is not supported by the text. First, the Greek word that the New Testament always uses to refer to the Torah (*nomos*) is nowhere to be found in this passage. Second, the idea that Messiah took away the Torah doesn't fit with Paul's argument. How would getting rid of the Torah assure forgiveness of sins? A better interpretation is that the "record of debt that stood against us with its legal demands" refers to the record of our sins. God's Torah legally demands death as payment from those who break it. However, the Messiah has canceled our record of sins that stood against us. If we have no sins being held against us, then we have nothing to be punished for—no legal demands that need to be satisfied. The Messiah did not cancel the law, but rather canceled the written record of *our transgressions of the law*, because he provided forgiveness for the sins that we had committed.

By canceling the record of our sins, the Messiah "disarmed the rulers and authorities and put them to open shame, by triumphing over them" (Colossians 2:15). That is, he has removed any power these spiritual forces might have had over us. Therefore, we need not seek out the wisdom or protection from any inferior spiritual entities. The Messiah has already provided everything we need.

Now that we have a better understanding of the Colossian heresy, and Paul's answer to it, let's turn again to Paul's admonition concerning certain Torah commandments:

> Therefore let no one pass judgment on you in questions of
> food and drink, or with regard to a festival or a new moon or
> a Sabbath. These are a shadow of the things to come, but the
> substance belongs to Christ.
> —Colossians 2:16-17

Once again, this passage is traditionally interpreted to mean that the Sabbath, festivals, etc., are now irrelevant in light of the Messiah. Therefore, the Colossian believers should not be judged for not observing them. But based on what we have learned about the false teachings Paul is dealing with, it seems clear that there is more going on here. Paul does not state that *the commandments* are invalid; he states that *the judgment of these false teachers* is invalid. A better understanding, which is consistent with the context, is that the Colossian believers are not to accept judgment from these false teachers regarding *how* to observe these commandments.[15] Why? Because the false teachers at Colossae applied esoteric meanings and ascetic rituals to these Torah command-ments (Colossians 2:21-22) and judged those who didn't follow their teachings (Colossians 2:16). Paul says their judgment is invalid. Their form of "Torah observance" is really no Torah observance at all. It is a false religion mixed with a distorted misuse of the Torah.

The scholar Douglas Moo likewise has recognized that Paul refers to aspects of the Torah that have been mixed with a broader religious philosophy in Colossians:

> On the whole, then, it seems best to view the practices in v. 16 as basically Jewish in origin and perhaps even orientation while still recognizing that they have been taken up into a larger mix of religious ideas and practices.[16]

---

15   See Caleb Hegg, *Instruction for Community, Family, & Personal Living: A Commentary on Colossians & Philemon* (Growing in Messiah, 2021), 71: "We should remember that Paul has called the Colossian heresy 'philosophy,' 'empty deceit,' and 'traditions of me' (v. 8). This is not how Paul talks about the law of God in other places. Rather, it seems more likely that those who oppose the Colossians are accusing the Church of failing to observe such things correctly. In verse 18, Paul references 'asceticism and worship of angels...' These are things that are clearly outside the biblical commands. Thus, Paul seems to be attacking those who are attempting to delegitimize the Colossian community for not worshiping in a specific way."

16   Douglas Moo, *Pillar New Testament Commentary: The Letters to the Colossians and to Philemon* (Grand Rapids, MI: Eerdmans, 2008), 221.

In other words, proper observance of these Torah commands was not the problem in Colossians. The problem was that false teachers had mixed things like the Sabbath and festivals with their mystical teachings.[17] Paul's admonition to the Colossian believers, then, is not to accept judgment on these matters from these false teachers. These false teachers misuse and distort the biblical commandments in their worship of various cosmic powers over which the Messiah has triumphed (Colossians 2:15). The problem was the perversion of these Torah commands within a false religious philosophy, not the commands themselves. Peter O'Brien puts it well:

> For Israel the keeping of these holy days was evidence of
> obedience to God's law and a sign of her election among the
> nations. At Colossae, however, the sacred days were to be kept
> for the sake of the "elemental spirits of the universe," those
> astral powers who directed the course of the stars and relegated
> the order of the calendar. **So Paul is not condemning the use
> of sacred days or seasons as such; it is the wrong motive
> involved when the observance of these days is bound up
> with the recognition of the elemental spirits.** [Emphasis
> added][18]

---

17   See A. T. Lincoln, *Colossians: New Interpreters Bible*, Vol. 11 (Abington Press, 2000), 631: "Again there is no hint here that such special days are being observed because of the desire to obey Torah as such or because keeping them was a special mark of Jewish identity. Instead, it is probable that in the philosophy they were linked to a desire to please the cosmic powers, the 'elemental spirits of the universe' (vv. 8, 20), held to be associated with the heavenly bodies and, therefore, in control of the calendar. Sabbath observance would have been no exception to this. Elchasai would later teach his followers that the sabbath was to be observed because it was one of the days controlled by the course of the stars."

18   Peter T. O'Brien, *Word Biblical Commentary: Colossians, Philemon* (Nashville, TN:

This added context clarifies what Paul means in verse 17. Paul says that things like the Sabbath and festivals serve as shadows pointing toward "the things to come, but the substance belongs to Christ." That is, these aspects of the Torah ultimately are intended to reveal the work of Messiah. Notice that Paul says these Torah commandments are a shadow of "things to come," not just things that have already happened. These commands function not only in memorializing Yeshua's work of atonement on the cross but also continue to point forward to his future work to occur at the end of the age. As Hegg writes, "Paul's point is that these Torah commandments are not the end in themselves, but are signposts pointing forward to Yeshua's final reign and victory."[19] Paul's ultimate point is that the Sabbath, festivals, etc., are intended to point beyond themselves to the Messiah, who is the substance. Commandments like the Sabbath are intended to be used to worship *the Messiah*, not inferior spiritual beings like angels.

In summary, a contextual understanding of Colossians 2:16-17 implies that Paul does not regard things like the Sabbath and festivals as unimportant. He condemns only a misuse of these laws in connection with mystical false teachings that downplay the Messiah and his work. The problem in Colossae was human precepts and teachings, not God's commandments themselves (Colossians 2:8, 22). However, when we observe commandments like the Sabbath appropriately, with a focus on the Messiah and his work of redemption, then there is no problem. In fact, recognizing that the "shadows" ultimately point to the Messiah ought to help us see the worth and significance of these shadows that much more.

Thomas Nelson, 1982), 139.

19   Hegg, *Why We Keep Torah*, 64.

Romans 14:5 — A Matter of Opinion

In Romans 14:5, Paul says that Christians have liberty to "esteem all days alike." Should we interpret this statement to mean that Sabbath observance is optional for Christians? When we examine this verse in context, we see that Paul is not addressing the Sabbath in this passage but something else entirely.

To begin, in Romans 14, Paul admonishes his readers not to pass judgment on one another over days and foods:

> One person believes he may eat anything, while the weak
> person eats only vegetables. Let not the one who eats despise
> the one who abstains, and let not the one who abstains pass
> judgment on the one who eats, for God has welcomed him.
> —Romans 14:2-3

> One person esteems one day as better than another, while
> another esteems all days alike. Each one should be fully
> convinced in his own mind. The one who observes the day,
> observes it in honor of the Lord. The one who eats, eats in
> honor of the Lord, since he gives thanks to God, while the one
> who abstains, abstains in honor of the Lord and gives thanks
> to God.
> —Romans 14:5-6

> Therefore let us not pass judgment on one another any longer,
> but rather decide never to put a stumbling block or hindrance
> in the way of a brother. I know and am persuaded in the Lord
> Jesus that nothing is unclean in itself, but it is unclean for
> anyone who thinks it unclean.
> —Romans 14:13-14

Based on these passages, should we assume that Paul is teaching that God doesn't care about whether or not believers observe the Sabbath and dietary laws in the Torah? Should we believe that Paul is saying here that a person who observes these commandments is "weak in faith" because observing them is unnecessary, and the important thing is that we don't judge each other or cause one another to stumble over these issues? There is no question that Paul says believers ought not to judge each other over days and foods and that one has the liberty to "eat anything" and "esteem all days alike." But the text is not clear on what is being addressed. Is Paul referring to the Torah's dietary laws and holy days, such as the command against eating pork and the command to rest on the Sabbath? Or is he referring to something else?

Many have assumed that Paul *must* be referring to the Torah's dietary laws and holy days in Romans 14. And if we read this chapter in isolation, then that might be a reasonable assumption. But such a view is difficult to reconcile with both the broader context of Romans and what we know about Paul from elsewhere in the New Testament.

First, as we have covered previously, Paul regularly observed the Sabbath throughout his ministry. Paul's faithful Sabbath observance is not what we would expect from someone who thought observing it was a sign of weak faith. On the other hand, Paul's actions *are* what we would expect from someone who believed that the Sabbath still ought to be kept.

Second, in Romans itself, Paul affirms the Torah's enduring validity. He declares that our faith does not overthrow but rather establishes the Torah (Romans 3:31). He teaches that sin is defined as breaking the Torah's commandments (Romans 7:7) and admonishes believers not to continue living in sin (Romans 6:1-2). He calls the Torah holy, righteous, and good (Romans 7:12). He calls the Torah spiritual (Romans 7:14) and says he delights in it (Romans 7:22). He says the Holy Spirit empowers believers to keep the Torah (Romans 8:2-4). These types of statements are not what we would expect from someone who believed the Sabbath and dietary laws were no longer important.

Third, we have Paul's direct testimony on this issue. When he spoke to the local Jewish leaders in Rome, we read that he assured them, "I had done nothing against our people or the customs of our fathers" (Acts 28:17). So, Paul testifies that he has never taught against the Jewish people or their "customs," which would undoubtedly include things like the Sabbath and dietary laws. The Jewish leaders in Rome admit, "We have received no letters from Judea about you, and none of the brothers coming here has reported or spoken any evil about you" (Acts 28:21). If Paul really taught the believers in Rome that they were free to disregard things like the Sabbath and dietary laws, surely the Jewish leadership in Rome would have heard about it. However, they said they hadn't heard anybody speak against Paul. Not only that, but Paul would be blatantly lying in Acts 28:17 if he *did* teach what many accuse him of teaching!

For these and other reasons, we shouldn't be so quick to jump to the conclusion that Paul must be referring to the Sabbath and dietary laws in Romans 14. As we have seen, that interpretation is inconsistent with Paul's teachings and actions elsewhere in Scripture. There is a better interpretation that doesn't require Paul to contradict himself and makes better sense of the context and specific language used in Romans 14. The opening verse gives us an important clue in understanding what Paul is addressing:

> As for the one who is weak in faith, welcome him, but not to quarrel over **opinions**.
> —Romans 14:1, emphasis added

The first thing to note is that there are two groups involved in this conflict. Paul refers to them as the "strong" and the "weak" (Romans 15:1). Here, Paul says to the strong that they are to welcome those who are weak in faith, but not as an invitation to quarrel over opinions. The verb for "welcome" (*proslambanō*) here means to receive someone into your home or group (cf. Acts 28:2). In verse 3, Paul reminds both groups that God has welcomed them, so they should welcome each other. Scholars widely identify the "strong" in this section as mainly Gentile believers, and the "weak" as mainly Jewish believers, which will make sense as we continue.

Second, Paul was addressing matters of "opinion." These were not matters of settled law that believers in Rome were quarreling over. While most Christians in modern times might think of things like the Sabbath and dietary laws as matters of opinion, that wasn't the case in Paul's day. There were certainly debates regarding *how* to observe some commandments in the Torah, but everyone recognized the commandments themselves as valid and authoritative. As we will see in chapter 3, the earliest evidence we have of Christians beginning to abandon commandments like the Sabbath is from the second century, long after the time of Paul.

Third, even though Paul had his own opinion about which side of this issue was correct (Romans 14:14), he does not seem to take a side in this debate. Instead, he indicates that the opinions on either side are to be tolerated. What Paul encourages here is unity and mutual understanding *despite* differences of opinion. Neither side is to judge the other because God has welcomed them both (Romans 14:3). This should make it obvious that the issues Paul deals with here are not matters of sin. As noted earlier, Paul defines sin as breaking the commandments of the Torah (Romans 7:7) and admonishes believers not to continue living in sin (Romans 6:1-2). It would be strange for Paul, in the same letter, to say that God welcomes those who reject his commandments.

So, what are the differences of *opinion* between these two groups? Paul addresses two issues: foods and days. We will spend some time exploring the issue of foods first. This will be helpful in establishing that Paul is not addressing commandments in this chapter. If it can be shown that Paul is talking about something different from God's commandments when he refers to foods, then it is also reasonable to conclude that he is not talking about the Sabbath when he refers to days. Here is what Paul says regarding foods:

> One person believes he may eat anything, while the weak
> person eats only vegetables.
> —Romans 14:2

As we can see, Paul is addressing a conflict between those who believe they may eat "anything" and those who eat only vegetables. The word "anything" must not be taken out of context. Again, these are matters of opinion, not commandments (Romans 14:1). So "anything" must mean any *biblically permitted* foods. Some other people, Paul says, avoid more than just the meats prohibited by the Torah. That is, they have restricted their diet to exclude meat entirely. This isn't a diet the Torah requires. The Torah prohibits eating meat only from unclean animals, not all animals. So, the difference of opinion was that some people believed that they could eat anything that the Bible permitted, while others believed that they should avoid some biblically-permitted foods, particularly meat (and wine, as we see in verse 21).

Why did some believers feel that they should eat only vegetables? The reason is that vegetarianism was an easy way to avoid potentially eating meat that some considered *koinos*. *Koinos* is a word that is usually translated as "common" in the New Testament, and unfortunately, it is also sometimes translated as "unclean." Here is where we need to bring out some important, often-overlooked details in this conflict that Paul is addressing. Later in the chapter, Paul says, "I know and am persuaded in the Lord Jesus that nothing is unclean in itself, but it is unclean for anyone who thinks it unclean" (Romans 14:14). The word translated as "unclean" in that verse is the Greek *koinos*. The important thing about the word *koinos* is that it does not mean biblically unclean. When the New Testament and Septuagint speak of unclean meats per the Torah's dietary laws, the word used is *akathartos*. If Paul were referring to meat from unclean animals in Romans 14, we would expect him to use the less ambiguous term *akathartos*, but he doesn't. He uses *koinos*. While this word is usually translated as "common," when used in the context of food or eating, it specifically denotes ritual impurity.[20]

Again, there is a significant difference between food that is *koinos*, that is, ritually impure, and food that is *akathartos*, that is, prohibited by God's commandments. In the minds of many first century Jews, foods could be considered *koinos*—ritually impure—for various reasons. Many of the reasons for considering certain foods *koinos* were not derived from explicit biblical commandments, as we will see. Regardless, if food was deemed *koinos*, many Jews considered it unacceptable for food, even though it was acceptable for food by biblical standards.

For instance, we see the word *koinos* used in the context of eating biblically permitted food during Yeshua's confrontation with the Pharisees in Mark 7. The Pharisees criticized Yeshua's disciples for neglecting their hand-washing rituals. The Pharisees asked, "Why do your disciples not walk according to the tradition of the elders, but

---

20 F. W. Gingrich, "Koinos," *Shorter Lexicon of the Greek New Testament* (Chicago, IL: University of Chicago Press, 1965), 118.

eat with defiled hands?" (Mark 7:5). The word "defiled" in this verse is *koinos*. From the Pharisees' perspective, eating with ritually impure hands made the food one was eating ritually impure as well. While the Torah does command priests to wash their hands when serving in the tabernacle (Exodus 30:17-21), there is no commandment for non-priests outside of the tabernacle to wash their hands before eating. In fact, Scripture explicitly identifies the Pharisees' ritual as "tradition," not a commandment (Mark 7:3-5).[21]

The point is this: the Torah does not say that clean food becomes ritually impure if you touch it with unwashed hands. That idea comes from later tradition. Nevertheless, many Jews of Yeshua's and Paul's day held to that tradition. This is important context to keep in mind when we see Yeshua and Paul seeming to disregard these matters of ritual purity. They were not disregarding biblical commandments, but rather man-made traditions. Again, *Koinos*, ritual impurity, is different from *akathartos*, the word for Torah-prohibited meats. However, there is a connection between the two terms. Peter uses both of these terms in Acts 10:

> The next day, as they were on their journey and approaching the city, Peter went up on the housetop about the sixth hour to pray. And he became hungry and wanted something to eat, but while they were preparing it, he fell into a trance and saw the heavens opened and something like a great sheet descending, being let down by its four corners upon the earth. In it

---

21 The Pharisees reinterpreted many of the commandments pertaining to the priesthood and temple and applied them outside of their original context. See Oskar Skarsaune, *In the Shadow of the Temple: Jewish Influences on Early Christianity* (Downers Grove, IL: IVP Academic, 2002), 121: "[T]he Pharisees sought to make every Israelite a priest and every meal a temple meal. Their aim was to extend the sanctity of the temple."

were all kinds of animals and reptiles and birds of the air. And
there came a voice to him: "Rise, Peter; kill and eat." But Peter
said, "By no means, Lord; for I have never eaten anything that
is common [koinos] or unclean [akathartos]."
—Acts 10:9-14

Peter describes the animals he sees in the vision as both *koinos*,
"common," and *akathartos*, "unclean." The fascinating thing about this
vision is that the sheet contained a mixture of clean and unclean animals.[22] What scholars have proposed is that *koinos* refers to clean animals that many Jews at the time saw as having become ritually defiled
by association with unclean animals.[23] According to Craig Keener:

> [T]he appearance of "all" animals in the sheet probably
> suggests that **they cannot be limited to either clean or
> unclean**. But some, at least, must be unclean (certainly the
> ἑρπετὰ [reptiles]), which explains Peter's reticence to eat them.
> The other, clean animals are not necessarily irrelevant either.
> It is probably not that Peter does not know how to butcher
> them in a kosher manner, in contrast to his tanner host; this
> ignorance would seem strange for a fisherman. **But if clean
> animals are present, their mixture with the unclean might**

---

22 See F. F. Bruce, *The Book of the Acts* (Grand Rapids, MI: Eerdmans, 1988), 206, n. 18:
"Peter might no doubt have slaughtered and eaten one of the 'clean' animals; but he
was scandalized by the unholy mixture of clean animals with unclean. This is specially
important in view of the practical way in which he had immediately to apply the lesson
of the vision."

23 For an in-depth study on this topic, see Colin House, "Defilement by Association: Some
Insights From the usage of KOINOS/KOINOU in Acts 10 and 11," *AUSS* (1983), Vol. 21,
No. 2: 143-153.

seem to contaminate them for a strict observer of kashrut.
[Emphasis added][24]

Ben Witherington also recognizes this point:

> [H]e refers to both the common (κοινὸν) and the unclean
> (ἀκάθαρτον). The former probably refers to something that
> could be defiled by association with something unclean, the
> latter to something inherently unclean. In other words, Peter
> assumed that because of the considerable presence of unclean
> animals and the possible problem of contamination, there was
> nothing fit to eat in the sheet.[25]

From the perspective of many Jews in Paul's day, some clean foods
could be rendered *koinos* through association with unclean animals.
This means that many Jewish believers at this time not only avoided
unclean meat per the Torah's dietary laws but also avoided any *clean
meat* that they regarded as having become ritually impure. This is similar to what we see in Mark 7. Some Jews would not eat food unless
they washed their hands first, per the tradition of the elders. Touching
food with ritually unwashed hands made the food *koinos*, even though
the food itself was clean by biblical standards.

There is one more thing to mention on this point. When we keep
reading Acts 10, we discover that the common and unclean animals
from Peter's vision were symbols representing Jews and Gentiles (Acts

---

24   Craig Keener, *Acts: An Exegetical Commentary, 3:1-14:28* (Grand Rapids: BakerAcademic,
     2013), 1769.

25   Ben Witherington III, *The Acts of the Apostles: A Socio-Rhetorical Commentary* (Grand
     Rapids, MI: Eerdmans, 1998), 350.

10:28). Many Jews during this time saw Gentiles as "unclean," and so they refused to fellowship with them out of concern that the Gentiles would cause them to become *koinos*—ritually impure—by association.[26] The vision helped Peter recognize that this mentality was entirely unbiblical and inappropriate:

> And he said to them, "You yourselves know how unlawful it is for a Jew to associate with or to visit anyone of another nation, but God has shown me that I should not call any person common [*koinos*] or unclean [*akathartos*].
> —Acts 10:28

When Peter says it is unlawful for Jews to associate with Gentiles, he is not referring to the Torah but to cultural taboos at the time. The Greek word for "unlawful" here is *athemitos*, which refers "not to what is forbidden by ordinance but to violation of tradition or common recognition of what is seemly or proper."[27] If this verse was referring to the Torah, the Greek word for "against the law" (*anomia*) would have been used. The Torah does not forbid Jews from fellowshipping or eating with Gentiles, but over time this became a cultural taboo. For instance, the Book of Jubilees, written around 100 BC, warns Jews against associating with Gentiles. It says, "Separate yourself from

---

26   See House, "Defilement by Association," 151: "Prior to the time of Christ, an extension of [Leviticus 20:24-26] had developed. In order to avoid inevitable contact with the symbol, Jewish tradition added to the OT stipulation by eventually regarding association with Gentile human beings themselves as a source of defilement. It is in this context that Peter's understanding of the term 'common' is intelligible."

27   Walter Bauer, *A Greek-English Lexicon of the New Testament and Other Early Christian Literature*, rev. and ed. Frederick W. Danker, 4th ed. (Chicago: University of Chicago Press, 2021), 21.

the gentiles, and do not eat with them."[28] This attitude is reflected in some Jews' criticism of Peter after he ministered to Gentiles. They said to him, "You went to uncircumcised men and ate with them" (Acts 11:3). From their perspective, Peter had made himself *koinos* through his association with the "unclean" Gentiles. But this attitude toward Gentiles directly conflicted with the heart of the Great Commission, which demanded making disciples of "all nations" (Matthew 28:19), hence the need for Peter to get over his prejudices.

Nevertheless, these cultural sentiments ran deep within early Judaism. Not only did many Jews avoid fellowshipping and eating with Gentiles but also avoided eating any meats or drinking any wine that came from Gentile sources (Romans 14:21). It was believed that foods and drinks handled by "unclean" Gentiles were rendered ritually impure by association, and therefore became unacceptable for consumption by Jews.[29] There is an abundance of historical evidence that shows Jews restricting their diet when Gentiles were in positions of control over food preparation.[30] Again, these ritual purity standards concerning food handled by Gentiles are nowhere to be found in the Torah itself.

---

28   Jubilees 22:16. Quoted in Keener, *Acts*, 1778.

29   See T. C. Smith, *Acts: The Broadman Bible Commentary* (Nashville, TN: 1970), 10.67: "The separatist policy in Judaism became so strict that oil, bread, milk, and meat could not be purchased from Gentiles. To eat pagan food was an abomination, but to dine in the house of a pagan was much worse."

30   For instance, the apocryphal book of Judith, dated between 135-78 BC, records that Judith brought her own wine, oil, grain, fruit, and bread when going to the Assyrian camp and dining with Nebuchadnezzar's general, Holofernes (Judith 10:5; 12:2, 19). In the book of Tobit, written between 225-175 BC, we see that Tobit also refused to eat the food of the Ninevites after he was taken into captivity (Tobit 1:10-11). Josephus mentions Jewish priests he knew who ate only figs and nuts when they were in Rome (Josephus, *Life of Flavius Josephus* 14). In the later rabbinic literature, we also see regulations governing the interactions between Jews and Gentiles that developed over time. Many of

Given these traditional Jewish purity standards regarding foods and drinks, it is no surprise when we get to the Book of Romans and see that some Jews were apprehensive about consuming meat and wine. Since the meat and wine would have been purchased from the public marketplace in Rome, many Jews would have considered them to be *koinos*. Jews would have felt this way for a few reasons: it is possible that some Jews suspected that the meat and wine were used in offerings to false gods—an issue Paul addresses directly in 1 Corinthians 8-10. Others might have suspected that the blood from the meat wasn't drained properly. Or, as suggested above, their apprehension simply might have been based on a ritual purity concern due to a deeply ingrained aversion toward foods and drinks handled by Gentiles. As E. P. Sanders writes:

> [B]ecause of ignorance, general suspicion, or the long-standing
> association of meat with sacrifice, Jews were reluctant to eat
> Gentile food, especially meat, just because it was Gentile.
> The objection, that is, may not have been technical—'it has
> blood in it'—but vague and traditional—'our family has never
> eaten Gentile meat' … Some Jews would eat Gentile meat if
> they could receive the right assurances about it, others simply
> would not eat it because it was Gentile.[31]

With this context in mind, Paul's statements about "unclean" foods in this chapter make a lot more sense. He is not talking about unclean

---

these regulations prohibit Jews from eating foods and drinking wine handled by Gentiles (m.*Tahorot* 7; m.*Avodah Zarah* 2, 4-5).

31 E. P. Sanders, *Jewish Law from Jesus to the Mishnah* (Philadelphia, PA: Trinity Press International, 1990), 279-280.

meats per the Torah's dietary laws, but rather meat that is *koinos*—that is, "clean animals which are somehow objectionable as food."[32] He is not saying that the Torah's standards of diet are irrelevant. Rather, he says he doesn't consider anything *koinos* in itself—that is, he doesn't consider *clean meats* purchased from Gentile sources to be ritually impure and unsuitable for food. In other words, as Colin House puts it, "nothing within the parameters of 'clean' food should be thought of as being made 'common.'"[33] However, Paul does say that such clean meat is *koinos* for anyone who thinks of it as *koinos* (Romans 14:14). That is, some believers, because they are "weak in faith," have genuine doubts about whether it is okay to consume certain foods and drinks due to ritual purity concerns. Therefore, when they attend fellowship meals, they might be seen eating only vegetables instead of partaking in the meat and wine (Romans 14:2). Paul says to welcome these believers (Romans 14:1).

One could see why this was such a controversy in Rome! This conflict was rooted in long-standing tensions between Jews and Gentiles. On one side, you had some Jews refusing to eat "Gentile food" because they feared it would make them ritually impure. How do you think

---

32   Clinton Wahlen, "Peter's Vision and Conflicting Definitions of Purity," *NTS* 51 (2005): 512. "Additional support for κοινόν having this sense may be found in 4 Macc 7.6, where the cognate verb (κοινόω) is used in praising Eleazar, who did not 'make himself common by eating defiled food.' The author describes attempts to persuade Eleazar to compromise his fidelity to the food laws, the last of which involves not the eating of pork but meat from a *clean* animal. Eleazar is asked to pretend that it is pork, which would clearly be out of the question for this pious Jew. Nevertheless, the designation of the meat as 'defiled food' is significant. Apparently even clean meat, if received from a Gentile and so presumably offered to idols, could be potentially defiling. The term κοινα is singularly appropriate to describe such doubtfully pure food, the acceptability of which could not be assured."

33   House, "Defilement by Association," 153.

that made Gentile believers feel? Probably like they were being judged and looked down on as unclean. On the other side, you had Gentile believers enjoying "ritually impure" meat and wine in the presence of their Jewish brothers, which probably made some Jews feel very uncomfortable.

From Paul's perspective, even though he is persuaded that nothing is *koinos* in itself, this is not an issue to divide over. In fact, he encourages his readers—those he calls "strong" (Romans 15:1)—to be especially considerate toward the weak, even if it means not eating meat or drinking wine in front of them (Romans 14:13-23; 15:1-6). Based on the historical tensions between Jews and Gentiles that we see throughout the New Testament, Paul probably sees it as a miracle that Jewish and Gentile believers are gathering together to begin with. He doesn't think it is worth possibly messing all of that up over this disagreement regarding ritual purity. If Jews are joining Gentiles for fellowship meals, they have already come a long way. Perhaps, as they continue to grow in faith, like Paul, they will be persuaded that nothing is *koinos* in itself. Regardless, Paul says not to let this issue destroy the fellowship. He tells the "strong" that they "have an obligation to bear with the failings of the weak" (Romans 15:1).

Now let's look at the second issue dividing believers at Rome, which was a difference of opinion concerning "days." Just like God accepts people on both sides of the "foods" debate, Paul states that God also accepts those on both sides of the "days" debate. According to Paul, this is not an issue to divide over:

> One person esteems one day as better than another, while
> another esteems all days alike. Each one should be fully
> convinced in his own mind.
> —Romans 14:5

Is Paul talking about the Torah's holy days like the Sabbath in this verse? That is unlikely for a couple of reasons. First, Paul never explicitly mentions the Sabbath or holy days anywhere in Romans, which should at least give us some pause before concluding the Torah's holy days must be the subject here. Second, as we have seen with regard to the issue of "foods" in this chapter, whatever the specific issue was, it was within the realm of opinions, not commandments (Romans 14:1). First-century Jews and Christians never considered holy days like the Sabbath mere matters of opinion. And as noted earlier, Christians didn't start abandoning commandments like the Sabbath until the second century, long after Romans was written.

There is better option for how to interpret the "days" mentioned in Romans 14:5. Many have proposed that Paul is addressing traditional fast days. Notably, some early church fathers, such as Augustine (*Letter 36*, to Casulanus) and John Chrysostom (*Homilies on Romans* 25), have interpreted these verses in Romans as applying to designated days of fasting. Some modern scholars mention this option as well.[34]

How likely is it that the conflict in Romans 14 was over traditional fast days? Based on biblical and historical evidence, it seems quite likely. We know that the Pharisees were known for fasting twice a week (Luke 18:12), and the rabbinic literature discusses setting aside Monday and Thursday for fasting (Tosefta to m. *Ta'anit* 2:4). So, it appears that fasting twice a week was a common practice. In contrast to the Pharisaic practice of fasting Monday and Thursday, the Didache, an early second-century Christian document, instructs its Gentile readers not to fast on the same days as "the hypocrites," but to fast on Wednesday

---

34   Tim Hegg, *Paul's Epistle to the Romans: Chapters 9-16* (Tacoma, WA: TorahResource, 2007), 412-417; J.K. McKee, *The New Testament Validates Torah: Does the New Testament Really Do Away With the Law?* (Richardson, TX: Messianic Apologetics, 2012), 229-253.

and Friday instead (Didache 8:1). For whatever reason, the writer to the Didache community thought that fasting on the traditional days of Monday and Thursday was associated with hypocritical people. Toby Janicki offers a suggestion on why that might be:

> The Didache instructs that followers of Messiah are to fast on Wednesday and Friday instead of on Monday and Thursday. These days are offered as sectarian alternatives to normative Jewish practice. It is possible that at certain times and places the fast days of Monday and Thursday were dominated by individuals looking to make a show of their righteousness. Fasting on the alternate days of Wednesday and Friday further safeguarded against making fasting an ostentatious show of piety, because no one in the broader Jewish community would suspect anyone of fasting then.[35]

In any case, it is clear from the Didache that there were indeed historical controversies regarding which days to fast. At least one early Christian community differed from the normative Jewish practice. The author of the Didache associated the practice of fasting on the traditional days of the week with hypocrites, and commanded that the Didache community fast on different days of the week. Thus, since we know that there were controversies over fast days between some groups, it is not unreasonable to think that the conflict Paul was addressing in Romans had to do with designated days of fasting. This option seems plausible in light of the very next verse. Paul connects designated days with "eating" and "abstaining":

---

35   Toby Janicki, *The Didache: A New Translation and Messianic Jewish Commentary* (Marshfield, MO: Vine of David, 2017), 308-309.

The one who observes the day, observes it in honor of the
Lord. The one who eats, eats in honor of the Lord, since he
gives thanks to God, while the one who abstains, abstains in
honor of the Lord and gives thanks to God.
—Romans 14:6

This verse seems to say that one's observance or non-observance of
the day is defined by their eating or abstaining—that is, whether or not
they fast. In either case, they give thanks to God. It is easy to see how
some might have judged others for fasting or not fasting on particular
days in light of the historical controversies regarding this issue. However, Paul says this difference of opinion is not worth dividing over.
He encourages the believers in Rome to love and welcome each other
despite their differences of opinion over traditions and issues that aren't
clearly mandated in the Scriptures.

In summary, Romans 14 does not teach that God doesn't care
whether or not believers observe the commanded Sabbath and dietary
laws. Both the broader context of Romans and the things we know
about Paul from elsewhere in the New Testament preclude such an
interpretation. When we examine this passage closely, a much more
likely interpretation emerges: the conflict over foods had to do with
concerns over ritual purity, and the conflict over days had to do with
traditional days of fasting. In both cases, Paul is addressing matters
of opinion, not commandments. Therefore, since the issues in Rome
did not concern obedience to the clear commands of Scripture, Paul
doesn't take a side. While he had his own opinions, he tolerates the
opinions different from his own. He encourages his readers to do the
same in hopes that the fellowship at Rome could be united in Messiah,
despite their differences.

Galatians 4:8-11 — Slaves to Days

In Galatians 4:10, Paul criticizes his readers for "observ[ing] days and months and seasons and years." Should this verse be interpreted as Paul condemning God's commanded holy days? That understanding is unlikely for numerous reasons.

The important thing to note is that Paul's readers in Galatians are former pagans: "Formerly, *when you did not know God*, you were enslaved to those that by nature are not gods" (Galatians 4:8, emphasis added). When Paul's readers were pagans, they would have observed *pagan* days and festivals. Such pagan observances are what Paul criticizes his readers for wanting to return to: "But now that you have come to know God, or rather to be known by God, how can you *turn back again* to the weak and worthless elementary principles of the world, whose slaves you want to be once more?" (Galatians 4:9, emphasis added). As Keener writes, "Pagan religion was festive and communal, which might offer temptations to turn back."[36]

Why would returning to pagan days and festivals be a problem? Troy Martin explains, "Because of its association with idolatry and false deities, marking time according to this pagan scheme is tantamount to rejecting Paul's Gospel and the one and only true God it proclaims."[37] Just as the biblical festival calendar revolves around the God of Israel and his saving acts in history, pagan calendars had their own religious festivals and rituals. Committing to the gospel involves rejecting idolatry—which includes not participating in pagan festival observances that had idolatrous associations. Again, according to the immediate context,

---

36 Craig Keener, *New Cambridge Bible Commentary: Galatians* (Cambridge University Press, 2018), 193.

37 Troy Martin, "Pagan and Judeo-Christian Time-Keeping Schemes in Gal 4.10 and Col 2.16," *New Testament Studies* (1996), Vol. 42, 117.

Paul does not condemn the biblical holy days in this passage; he condemns the religious days of the pagans. As Hegg explains:

> [T]hat Paul is referring to pagan days, months, seasons, and years fits best with the language he uses in which he speaks of the Gentiles as "turning back again" (ἐπιστρέφετε, *epistrefete*) to the weak and worthless elements. He has already identified their past as that of idolatry (v. 8). To use the term "turn back again" for those whose former life was one of idolatry helps us identify that to which they were tempted to turn.[38]

Some reject this interpretation because Paul's argument throughout Galatians is against Jewish pressures to convert to Judaism. Paul's Jewish opponents in Galatians taught that the Gentiles' salvation and inclusion in the covenant community depended on becoming "Jewish" via ritual conversion (a process that involved getting circumcised) and that their "Jewish" status was maintained by Torah observance (as defined by the false teachers). Paul argues that submitting to this false teaching is a rejection of the true gospel, which teaches that salvation and inclusion in the covenant community are on the basis of faith, not on the basis of being Jewish.[39] Since the broader context of Galatians deals with Paul's repudiation of this false teaching taught by his Jewish opponents, some have seen the "days and months and seasons and

---

38 Tim Hegg, *Paul's Epistle to the Galatians* (Tacoma, WA: TorahResource, 2010), 188.

39 Paul's issue was not with the Torah but with a misuse of the Torah. The false teachers in Galatians were putting the proverbial cart before the horse. They said that one could earn their place in the world to come through human effort in accordance with their application of the Torah. Paul taught that true obedience to the Torah flows from genuine faith in the Messiah. For a fuller discussion on the context of Galatians, see my teaching, "Why Then The Law? (Galatians 3:19-29)" available at www.davidwilber.com.

years" in Galatians 4:10 as a reference to the Jewish (biblical) calendar. The argument is that the Gentiles embracing the Sabbath and holy days of the Torah *is like* turning back to paganism. However, this interpretation of Galatians 4:10 is problematic. After all, Paul himself observed and taught the Torah's holy days!

A better way to reconcile the apparent tension between this verse's immediate and broader context is to recognize that the Galatian believers were presented with a false choice. The false teachers in Galatians persuaded the Gentile believers that only two options were available to them: become Jewish via ritual conversion or go back to paganism. Because many Gentile believers refused to submit to ritual conversion, some were tempted to return to their former enslavement to false gods since they believed they had no other option. Thus, Paul condemns his opponents' false gospel for two reasons. First, he wants to prevent Gentile believers from submitting to ritual conversion to become "Jewish" for salvation. Why? Because this idea undermines the true gospel of salvation by faith. Second, he wants to prevent Gentile believers from leaving the faith entirely and returning to paganism. Refuting his opponents' false gospel "remove[s] the cause of the Galatians' apostasy to paganism."[40]

Paul's gospel gives the Gentile believers a much better option than the false choice presented to them by his opponents. Paul taught that the Gentile believers are already justified and included in the covenant community by virtue of their faith in the Messiah. Therefore, Paul urges his readers not to become enslaved to false beliefs again, whether that be by submitting to the false teaching of his opponents or by returning to their former ways of life in paganism. This understanding

---

40   Troy Martin, "Pagan and Judeo-Christian Time-Keeping Schemes in Gal 4.10 and Col 2.16," *New Testament Studies* (1996), Vol. 42, 116.

of Paul's argument "harmonizes the broader context of Galatians with the immediate context of Gal 4.10 without denying the validity of either."[41]

In summary, Paul's mention of "days and months and seasons and years" in Galatians 4:10 refers to pagan festival observances that would have had idolatrous associations. Paul's concern was that his readers, who were former pagans, might "turn back again" to these pagan days, months, seasons, and years because they were led to believe that returning to paganism was their only option if they refused to convert to Judaism. Paul addresses this false choice presented to his readers by emphasizing the true gospel, which teaches that the Gentile believers are already full members of God's family by virtue of their faith in the Messiah. Having refuted the idea that the Gentile believers must "convert or leave," in Galatians 4:8-11, Paul admonishes them not to return to paganism. Therefore, Galatians 4:10 does not condemn *biblical* holy days like the Sabbath. Rather, in accord with the immediate context of this verse, Paul condemned *pagan* festival observances.

Hebrews 3:7-4:11 — There Remains a Sabbath Rest

In Hebrews 4:9, the author of Hebrews says, "there remains a Sabbath rest for the people of God." Within the context of Hebrews 3:7-4:11, the "Sabbath rest" to which the author refers is the eternal rest for God's people in the world to come, which has been made available through the Messiah. We must "strive to enter that rest," which means remaining faithful to the Messiah and not falling "by the same sort of disobedience" (4:11) exhibited by the generation of Israelites under Moses who failed to enter the land because of their unbelief (3:7-18). In this passage, the author of Hebrews teaches that the Sabbath has a

---

41   Ibid., 116-117.

deeper meaning—it points to the ultimate rest promised to those who put their faith in the Messiah.

Does this passage imply a transformation of the Sabbath from a literal to a spiritual application? Some have suggested that because the Messiah offers us ultimate rest in the world to come, we now keep the Sabbath *spiritually* by believing in the Messiah and resting in his completed work. As A. T. Lincoln argues:

> What is the Sabbath rest that the New Testament people of God must observe? It is to enter God's rest and thereby cease from one's own works (4:10). This is analogous to God's ceasing from His works at the creation (cf. also 4:4). As we have seen, God's rest is entered by believing (4:3). Therefore the New Covenant people of God discharge their duty of Sabbath observance, according to this writer, by exercising faith.[42]

According to this perspective, since the literal commandment to rest on the seventh day was a shadow of the ultimate rest given to us in the Messiah, the shadow can now be discarded in light of the Messiah's salvific work. As John MacArthur argues, the Sabbath was "a sign and a symbol to lead the people to rest and repentance. But when you come to the New Testament, there's never a repeat of that command. The rest that the New Testament is concerned about is the rest that comes to the soul from hearing and believing the good news preached."[43]

---

42 A.T. Lincoln, "Sabbath, Rest, and Eschatology in the New Testament," *From Sabbath to Lord's Day: A Biblical, Historical, and Theological Investigation* (Grand Rapids, MI: Zondervan, 1982), 213.

43 John MacArthur, "Understanding the Sabbath," *Grace to You*. www.gty.org.

The Sabbath does indeed function as a symbol of the ultimate rest we have in the Messiah, but this fact does not do away with literal Sabbath observance. The idea that a commandment should be discarded when its deeper meaning is revealed is not logical nor consistent with anything else in the Bible. As Skip MacCarty puts it, the author of Hebrews does not "teach [faith in the Messiah] as a replacement for the literal observance of the Sabbath commandment, any more than Jesus intended His teaching on the deeper meaning of the commandments prohibiting murder and adultery to be interpreted as repealing a literal observance of those commandments."[44] Additionally, the Sabbath, like marriage, was established in creation (Hebrews 4:4; cf. Genesis 2:3). When Paul revealed the deeper meaning of marriage as a symbol for the church's relationship with Christ (Ephesians 5:31-33), he did not intend to teach that the literal marriage institution was now done away with. Why would we think that the author of Hebrews' teaching on the deeper meaning of the Sabbath did away with the literal commandment?

In reality, instead of repealing the Sabbath, this passage from Hebrews actually indicates that literal Sabbath observance is still expected of Christians. The word for "Sabbath rest" in Hebrews 4:9 is *sabbatismos*, which refers to the literal act of resting on the Sabbath day. Samuele Bacchiocchi writes that *sabbatismos* "is used several times as a technical term for Sabbathkeeping in post-canonical literature by Plutarch, Justin, Epiphanius, the *Apostolic Constitutions* and the *Martyrdom of Peter and Paul*."[45] A. T. Lincoln agrees that "the term denotes

---

44 Skip MacCarty, "Responses to Craig L. Bloomberg," *Perspectives on the Sabbath: 4 Views*, Christopher Donato, ed. (Nashville, TN: B& H Academic, 2011), 369.

45 Samuele Bacchiocchi, *The Sabbath in the New Testament* (Berrien Springs, MI: Biblical Perspectives, 2000), 50. Bacchiochi references Plutarch, *De Superstitione* 3 (Moralia 1660); Justin Martyr, *Dialogue with Trypho* 23, 3; Epiphanius, *Adversus Haereses* 30, 2, 2;

the observance or celebration of the Sabbath" and points out that it "corresponds to the Septuagint usage of the cognate verb *sabbatizo* (cf. Ex 16:23; Lev 23:32; 26:34f; 2 Chron 36:21), which also has reference to Sabbath observance."[46]

Thus, instead of being done away with, Sabbath rest (observance) "remains" for the people of God (Hebrews 4:9). This fact indicates that the author of Hebrews expects his readers to literally observe the Sabbath with its deeper meaning in mind. As Tim Hegg writes:

> [O]ur observance of the weekly Shabbat ought to have a
> far-reaching significance—one that has eternity in view.
> Indeed, the weekly Shabbat which we celebrate should, among
> other things, continually be a reminder of eternity and a means
> by which our faith is strengthened as we anticipate the return
> of our Messiah ... Clearly, then, this text of Hebrews, far from
> dismissing, or reinterpreting, or somehow re-appropriating
> the Torah commandment of Shabbat into something which is
> entirely personal, inward, and without outward observance is
> in every way foreign to our author's meaning and purpose.[47]

In summary, according to the author of Hebrews, the Sabbath has a deeper meaning—it symbolizes the ultimate rest that Christians have in the Messiah. While some have interpreted the author of Hebrews' teaching on the Sabbath as indicating that belief in the Messiah replaces

---

Apostolic Constitutions 2, 36.

46   A.T. Lincoln, "Sabbath, Rest, and Eschatology in the New Testament," *From Sabbath to Lord's Day: A Biblical, Historical, and Theological Investigation* (Grand Rapids, MI: Zondervan, 1982), 213.

47   Tim Hegg, *A Commentary on The Book of Hebrews Chapters 1-8* (Tacoma, WA: TorahResource, 2016), 167.

literal Sabbath observance, such a conclusion is a *non sequitur*.[48] Nobody believes that Yeshua's teachings on the deeper meanings of the commandments against murder and adultery did away with those literal commandments, or that Paul's teaching on the deeper meaning of marriage did away with the literal marriage institution. Thus, it does not make sense to think that the Sabbath's deeper meaning does away with literal Sabbath observance. Additionally, the meaning of the Greek word for "Sabbath rest" in Hebrews 4:9 indicates that literal Sabbath observance is still expected of Christians. As Christians, our Sabbath observance should remind us of the eternal rest we have in the Messiah.

Conclusion

In this chapter, we saw that Yeshua's confrontation with the Pharisees in Matthew 12:1-8 was over *how* to keep the Sabbath, not an example of Yeshua disregarding the Sabbath. Yeshua defended his disciples against the Pharisees' accusation that they broke the Sabbath and asserted his authority as the rightful interpreter of the commandment. We also learned that Colossians 2:16-17 does not imply that Paul thought of the Sabbath as unimportant. Instead, Paul condemned only a *misuse* of the Sabbath and festivals in connection with mystical false teachings, not those commandments themselves. In Romans 14, we saw that the conflict over days and foods that Paul addresses in the chapter had nothing to do with the Sabbath and dietary laws in the Torah; it had to do with man's *opinions* over ritual purity and designated fast days. In Galatians 4:10, we learned that Paul's mention of "days and months and seasons and years" refers to *pagan* festival observances, not biblical holy days like the Sabbath. Finally, when we examined Hebrews 4:9, we

---

48   Non Sequitur: "a conclusion or statement that does not logically follow from the previous argument or statement" (www.lexico.com/en/definition/non_sequitur).

saw that it does not indicate that Sabbath observance had been nullified in light of the Sabbath's deeper meaning. Instead, the Greek word for "Sabbath rest" suggests that literal Sabbath observance "remains" for God's people. Based on our examination of these passages from the New Testament, it is clear that the idea that the Sabbath was repealed is without a legitimate biblical basis.

CHAPTER 3

ANSWERING OBJECTIONS: SUNDAY HAS REPLACED THE SABBATH

Why don't most modern Christians observe the Sabbath? Many would answer that question by saying that the Sabbath was repealed. (I addressed the common arguments in support of that position in chapter 2.) Others, however, might respond to that question by saying, "What do you mean? I keep the Sabbath every *Sunday* when I attend church services!" Indeed, for many Christians, the Sabbath was not repealed, but it *was* changed.

The idea that the Sabbath commandment was reassigned to Sunday (the "Lord's day") is a popular opinion among modern Christians. For instance, the Westminster Confession states that the Sabbath "from the beginning of the world to the resurrection of Christ, was the last day of the week; and from the resurrection of Christ, was changed into the first day of the week, which, in Scripture, is called the Lord's Day and is to be continued to the end of the world, as the Christian Sabbath."[1]

However, while many modern Christians observe Sunday as the "Christian sabbath," the New Testament does not endorse this change. This chapter will demonstrate that the earliest Christians observed the Sabbath on the seventh day (Friday evening to Saturday evening). Additionally, we will see that the Sabbath's disappearance in Christianity was not universal but happened gradually over centuries for reasons

---

1   *Westminster Confession* XXI:VII

that were unrelated to biblical teaching. Finally, Sunday observance was not widely considered a replacement of the Sabbath in Christianity until long after the time of the apostles.

Evidence of Sunday Observance in the New Testament?

A survey of the Book of Acts reveals that while the earliest Christians met privately in homes,[2] they also remained connected to the religious calendar and practices of broader Judaism. They kept the Sabbath from Friday evening to Saturday evening and met together for fellowship in the synagogue[3] and temple[4] long after Yeshua's resurrection. As Lawrence Geraty writes:

> There is no evidence in the New Testament for any move on
> the part of Jesus' followers to replace the Jewish Sabbath. On
> the contrary, the Book of Acts describes the private gatherings
> of early Christians as not conflicting with the Temple or
> synagogue services, but rather as complementing them. These
> earliest Christians were known as Nazarenes (Acts 24:5),
> within the Jewish fold, similar to the Jewish parties of the
> Sadducees (Acts 5:17) and Pharisees (Acts 15:5; 26:5). There
> appears to be no desire to leave the parent religion.[5]

As I covered in chapter 1, the apostle Paul regularly worshiped in the synagogue on the Sabbath (Acts 13:13-52; 17:2; 18:4). Accord-

---

2 Acts 1:13; 2:46; 5:42; 12:12; 20:7.
3 Acts 9:20; 13:5, 14, 42; 14:1; 17:1, 10, 17; 18:4, 19, 26; 19:8.
4 Acts 2:46; 3:4; 5:12, 20, 25, 42.
5 Lawrence T. Geraty, "From Sabbath to Sunday: Why, How and When?" *Partings: How Judaism and Christianity Became Two*, Hershel Shanks, ed. (Washington, DC: Biblical Archaeology Society, 2013), 256.

ing to Acts 17:2, this was his "custom." The apostles themselves not only continued to worship in the synagogue on the Sabbath but also expected new Gentile Christians to attend Sabbath services regularly as well (Acts 15:21). As Herold Weiss writes, "The New Testament shows that the Sabbath occupied a prominent position in the early Christian communities."[6]

Based on everything we have learned so far in this book, it is clear that the earliest Christians continued to observe and meet on the seventh day, the Sabbath. But what evidence might the New Testament provide to suggest a change from the seventh day to the first day? As noted earlier, the Westminster Confession states that "from the resurrection of Christ, [the Sabbath] was changed into the first day of the week." But does the New Testament actually teach that the Messiah's resurrection changed the day of the Sabbath? Not at all.

While the Messiah rose from the dead on the first day of the week, the references to this day in the resurrection narratives are mere matter-of-fact statements, not announcements of a new holy day.[7] As MacCarty puts it, "There is no hint in any of these accounts of any

---

6   Herold Weiss, *A Day of Gladness: The Sabbath among Jews and Christians in Antiquity* (Columbia, SC: University of South Carolina Press, 2003), 177.

7   See Skip MacCarty, "The Seventh-Day Sabbath," *Perspectives on the Sabbath: 4 Views,* Christopher Donato, ed. (Nashville, TN: B& H Academic, 2011), 32-33: "In a matter-of-fact statement, Matthew specifies the time of Jesus' resurrection in these words: 'After the Sabbath, at dawn on the first day of the week' (28:1). Similar language is used in Mark 16:1-2, Luke 24:1, and John 20:1 for the timing of His resurrection. Mark 16:9-14 adds that He appeared later that same day to Mary Magdalene, to two others (cf. Luke 24:13-35), and to 'the Eleven' disciples. John adds that Jesus' visit to the disciples that day included His breathing on them that they might receive the Holy Spirit (20:19-23). John also records a visit Jesus made to the disciples 'a week later'...to show Himself to Thomas who had not been present at Jesus' first visit with the disciples and who doubted that He had been resurrected (20:26-29)."

expectation that 'the first day of the week' might have significance as a continuing worship day, replacing the Sabbath commandment."[8] To say that the Messiah's resurrection instituted Sunday as a replacement of the Sabbath (like John MacArthur argues[9]) is to read something into the text that simply isn't there.

What else in the New Testament might support the idea of replacing the seventh day with the first day? John MacArthur cites three passages that he believes establish a pattern of regular Christian Sunday observance: Acts 20:7, 1 Corinthians 16:1-2, and Revelation 1:10.[10] Do these passages uphold Sunday as the new "Christian Sabbath?" Let's begin with the verse from Acts:

> On the first day of the week, when we were gathered together
> to break bread, Paul talked with them, intending to depart on
> the next day, and he prolonged his speech until midnight.
> —Acts 20:7

This verse says that the believers met "on the first day of the week," broke bread, and listened to Paul speak. Does this verse declare that a shift from Sabbath observance to Sunday observance had already occurred among Christians? According to John MacArthur:

> And so, they met every day, but it didn't take long before
> **they landed on a special day** … "On the first day of the

---

8   Ibid., 33.

9   John MacArthur, "Why Sunday is the Lord's Day," *Grace to You*, www.gty.org: "The resurrection was the dawning of a new day, and so the new covenant has a new day. The Sabbath is gone, and the new day has come, and it is the day of celebration of the work of Christ."

10 Ibid.

week, when we were gathered together to break bread"—isn't that interesting? No law has been given to establish this. But here we are well into the ministry of the apostle Paul. Years have passed since the resurrection of Jesus Christ, and it's not remarkable, it's matter of fact: "When we were gathered together to break bread on the first day of the week." That's what they did … This church at Troas is exemplary of **the pattern of Sunday worship** in the early church and ever since. [Emphasis added][11]

As we can see, MacArthur thinks that this verse indicates a "pattern of Sunday worship." Now, even if it were true that these Christians regularly observed Sunday at this time, it still wouldn't prove that they abandoned Sabbath observance. All it would mean is that they started observing Sunday too.[12] Nevertheless, there are reasons to doubt that this gathering mentioned in Acts 20:7 gives us evidence of a pattern of Sunday observance. To state that this gathering was a recurring weekly meeting goes beyond the evidence. As Craig Keener writes, "Luke's note that the church was meeting on the first day could indicate a regular practice, *or it could point to a practice that was unusual* [emphasis added]."[13] While it may be a *possibility* that this was a weekly meeting, nothing in the text clearly suggests that it was. All the text tells us is

---

11   Ibid.

12   We have evidence from the 4-5th centuries of Christians observing both the Sabbath and Sunday (*Apostolic Constitutions* 7.23; Socrates Scholasticus, *Ecclesiastical History* 5.22; Sozomen, *Ecclesiastical History* 7.19), a practice maintained in some Christian communities today, such as the Ethiopian Church.

13   Craig Keener, *Acts: An Exegetical Commentary, 15:1-23:35* (Grand Rapids, MI: Baker Academic, 2014), 2963.

that Paul was "intending to depart on the next day," so the believers gathered to break bread and fellowship with Paul before he left.

Some might argue that since Luke, the author of Acts, seemingly goes out of his way to make special reference to the day in Acts 20:7, that this suggests it was a regular weekly gathering. However, that is not necessarily the case. As an eyewitness to Paul's journeys, Luke gives a chronological account of everything that happened. In chapters 20-21 alone, Luke "gives no less than thirteen time references to report the various stages of Paul's journey."[14] The mention of the first day of the week could simply have been "one of a whole series of chronological notes with which Luke fills the narrative of this voyage."[15] Also, it was at this meeting where the miracle of Eutychus being brought back to life occurred (Acts 20:8-12). Thus, the simplest explanation for Luke's reference to the first day of the week was not that this was a recurring Sunday meeting but rather, as Samuele Bacchiocchi writes, "(1) because Paul was 'ready to depart' (20:7), (2) because of the extraordinary experience and miracle of Eutychus, and (3) because it provides an additional significant chronological reference to describe the unfolding of Paul's journey."[16]

Could the mention of the breaking of bread be a reference to the commemoration of the Lord's Supper and indicate that the gathering in Acts 20:7 was a weekly meeting? Once again, that idea assumes too

---

14   Samuele Bacchiocchi, *From Sabbath to Sunday: A Historical Investigation of the Rise of Sunday Observance in Early Christianity* (Rome, Italy: The Pontifical Gregorian University Press, 1977), 103. Bacchiocchi cites Acts 20:3, 6, 7, 15, 16; 21:1, 4, 5, 7, 8, 10, 15, 18.

15   Ibid.

16   Ibid.

much. After all, the early believers "broke bread" together daily (Acts 2:46).[17]

Thus, unlike the Sabbath, which the Book of Acts clearly describes as a weekly meeting day that the apostles observed (e.g., Acts 17:2), nothing in the text of Acts 20:7 indicates that this Sunday meeting was a weekly occurrence.

What about 1 Corinthians 16:1-2?

> Now concerning the collection for the saints: as I directed the churches of Galatia, so you also are to do. On the first day of every week, each of you is to put something aside and store it up, as he may prosper, so that there will be no collecting when I come.
>
> —1 Corinthians 16:1-2

In this passage, Paul instructs the Corinthian believers to put aside funds on the first day of every week to help the poor believers in Jerusalem. This is often interpreted to mean that the believers met together on every Sunday, but is that accurate? There are good reasons we should doubt that interpretation.

First, Paul's letter to the Corinthians was written only a few years after he visited Corinth (Acts 18). The only reference to a customary meeting day in Corinth is the Sabbath: "After this Paul left Athens and went to Corinth...and he reasoned in the synagogue every Sabbath, and tried to persuade Jews and Greeks" (Acts 18:1, 4). Many of

---

17   See Robert K. McIver, "When, where, and why did the change from Sabbath to Sunday worship take place in the early church?" *AUSS*, Vol. 53, No. 1, 21-22: "The mention of 'breaking bread' in Acts 20:7 & 11, is likely to have been a reference to the celebration of the Lord's Supper, but this hardly indicates a weekly meeting, as at the time, it was not unknown for the early believers to 'break bread' together daily (e.g., Acts 2:46)."

the Corinthians accepted Paul's message and were baptized, including "Crispus, the ruler of the synagogue...together with his entire household" (Acts 18:8). We have no record of regular Sunday meetings in Corinth during or after Paul's extended stay, only Sabbath meetings (Acts 18:11). It seems unlikely that the early Christian community in Corinth (made up of both Jewish and Gentile believers) would have changed their day of worship only a few years after this account in Acts 18. As Norman Young writes:

> [A]ll forms of early Christianity were Jewish. Given this
> continuity with Judaism and the way in which communities
> tenaciously adhere to their holy days, it seems inconceivable
> that Jewish Christians shifted their worship over to meet with
> their fellow Gentile Christians on Sunday without so much
> as a murmur of protest ... It is inconceivable that Jewish
> Christians in the apostolic era were meeting on any other day
> than the Sabbath; and if they were to meet unitedly with the
> Gentile Christians, the latter had to join the former on the
> Sabbath and not Sunday.[18]

Second, nothing in the text of 1 Corinthians 16 indicates that the Corinthian believers made this donation at a public gathering. The instruction is for "each of you"—that is, each individual believer or household—to privately set aside funds. The instruction to "store it up" also implies keeping the funds in one's own home so that it could

---

18   Norman H. Young, "The Use of Sunday for Meetings of Believers in the New Testament':
      A Response," *Novum Testamentum* 45, no. 2 (2003): 116-117.

be easily gathered when Paul came for it.[19] It is not clear that any corporate gathering is in view at all.

Third, this reference to the first day of the week actually "should be considered evidence *against* any particular religious significance being attached to Sunday."[20] As McIver explains:

> Paul is urging his readers to consider their financial situation from the previous week. This makes sense if, in fact, the Christians at Corinth were observing Sabbath as a day free of work and financial considerations (i.e., were Sabbath-observant). In that case, the first day of the week would be the natural time for them to review their finances from the previous week, a type of business activity that was totally unsuited to a day of worship.[21]

Once again, there is no indication that the Corinthian believers changed their day of worship from the seventh day of the week to the first day of the week during or after Paul's extended stay in Corinth in Acts 18. Also, the text of 1 Corinthians 16:1-2 indicates that Paul was not instructing believers to set aside funds collectively but individually. Each believer was to set aside funds for the poor in Jerusalem. There would be no necessity for these believers to meet together to fulfill Paul's request. Lastly, the type of activity Paul instructs the Corinthian believers to engage in on the first day of the week may, in fact, be evidence *against* Sunday having religious significance to his readers.

---

19   See F. F. Bruce, *1 and 2 Corinthians* (London: Oliphants, 1971), 158: "each member is to put something aside *par*', 'at home,' and store it up there."

20   McIver, "When, where, and why...?" 20.

21   Ibid.

What about Revelation 1:10?

I was in the Spirit on the Lord's day, and I heard behind me a
loud voice like a trumpet.
—Revelation 1:10

Some suggest that John's mention of the "Lord's day" in Revelation 1:10 is a reference to Sunday, which would imply that Christians already considered Sunday a sacred day by John's time. However, is this interpretation based on any explicit biblical passage? Every time Sunday is mentioned in the New Testament, including in John's own gospel, it is not called "the Lord's day" but instead is referred to as "the first day of the week."[22] As A. M. Rodríguez writes, "It is particularly striking that John will use the traditional designation for Sunday in the gospel ["first day of the week"] and then in Revelation, written at approximately the same time, use a totally new name for Sunday; a name that as far as we know was not being used by the apostles to refer to Sunday."[23] Moreover, the only day that Scripture designates as "the Lord's" is the seventh-day Sabbath. Isaiah 58:13 calls the Sabbath "the holy day of the Lord." God refers to the Sabbath as "my Sabbath" sixteen times in the Old Testament.[24] All three synoptic gospels say that the Sabbath is the day of which Yeshua is "lord" (Matthew 12:8; Mark 2:28; Luke 6:5). Based purely on the biblical evidence, if we must choose between the Sabbath and Sunday, it seems that the Sabbath is a more likely candidate for being the "Lord's day."

---

22   Matthew 28:1; Mark 16:2, 9; Luke 24:1; John 20:1, 19; Acts 20:7; 1 Corinthians 16:2.

23   A. M. Rodríguez, "The Biblical Sabbath: The Adventist Perspective," *Biblical Research Institute General Conference of Seventh-day Adventists* (2002), 30.

24   Exodus 31:13; Leviticus 19:3; 30; 26:2; Deuteronomy 5:14; Isaiah 56:4, 6; Ezekiel 20:12, 13, 16, 20, 21, 24; 22:8; 23:38; 44:24.

Nevertheless, the argument has been made that "Lord's day" in Revelation 1:10 is referring to Sunday because Christian writers from the second century called Sunday "the Lord's day." As John MacArthur remarks:

> Now, when is John writing? Well, he's writing 30-40 years after Paul. He's writing in 96 A.D. at the end of the first century, and by that time this was no longer called Sunday, or whatever other forms that day had been called. It was for believers now the Lord's Day. It doesn't even need a further explanation. There are all kinds of testimonies in the second century—which would have been just a few years later since John's writing in 96—all kinds of testimonies to the fact that in the second century this was the customary way to refer to the first day of the week. The first day of the week was the Lord's Day; the day that we honor the Lord. This title for Sunday is commonly found in many, many early Christian writings, has continued through all church history, even down to the present.[25]

According to MacArthur, the apostle John is using the same terminology as Christian writings from the second century. Since those writings used the term "Lord's day" to refer to Sunday, when John wrote "Lord's day" in Revelation 1:10, he was also referring to Sunday. Therefore, by the time Revelation was written, Christians were already observing Sunday as a sacred day.

Does the historical evidence substantiate these claims? The writings that use the term "Lord's day" with clear reference to Sunday

---

25   John MacArthur, "Why Sunday is the Lord's Day," *Grace to You*, www.gty.org.

ANSWERING OBJECTIONS: SUNDAY HAS REPLACED THE SABBATH

were not written until more than half a century after John wrote the book of Revelation. As MacCarty points out, "The first unambiguous use of 'Lord's' (*kuriake*) with the noun 'day' in reference to Sunday occurs somewhere between AD 150 and 190 in the apocryphal *Gospel of Peter*, but it refers to the actual day of Christ's resurrection and not to a weekly day of worship."[26] Another occurrence of the term "Lord's Day" with reference to Sunday appears between AD 180-190 in the apocryphal *Acts of Peter*. This occurrence does seem to indicate a weekly religious observance, "but it also refers to the Sabbath as a day people brought their sick to be healed."[27] In any case, the fact that later writings connect the term "Lord's day" to Sunday does not necessarily mean that John meant Sunday when he used this term in Revelation 1:10. It would be anachronistic to interpret John's use of this term in accordance with such late evidence. As MacCarty writes:

> The historical records reveal that the first unambiguous connection between "Lord's Day" and Sunday does not show up in Christian literature until the second half of the second century, many decades after John used the term. Therefore, it is clear that those who interpret the "Lord's Day" in Rev 1:10 as Sunday do this on the basis of extrabiblical evidence that is much later than the time when John wrote Revelation. This is an unsound methodology of biblical interpretation.[28]

---

26   MacCarty, "The Seventh-Day Sabbath," 37. MacCarty cites *The Gospel of Peter* 9:35, 12:50; *New Testament Apocrypha*, ed. W. Schneemelcher (Cambridge: J. Clarke, 1991), 1:221, 224-25.

27   Ibid. MacCarty cites *Acts of Peter*, 1, 29-31; *New Testament Apocrypha*, 2:283, 285, 311-12.

28   Ibid.

With that said, there are two writings from the early second century that are worthy of comment: the *Didache* (AD 100) and Ignatius's *letter to the Magnesians* (AD 115). These texts were written much closer to the time when Revelation was written, and they are often cited as early evidence of the term "Lord's day" being used to refer to Sunday.[29] However, the way the term is used in these two writings is ambiguous, as we will see.

Let's first consider the Didache, a short treatise on morality and church practices from an anonymous Christian author. Here is the relevant passage:

On every Lord's Day—his special day—come together and
break bread and give thanks, first confessing your sins so
that your sacrifice may be pure. Anyone at variance with his
neighbor must not join you, until they are reconciled, lest your
sacrifice be defiled.
—Didache 14:1-2[30]

According to this translation of the passage, it seems clear that the early Christian community to whom the Didache was written gathered on "every Lord's Day." Is this evidence of early Christian Sunday

---

29   Richard Bauckham gives a list of thirteen second-century writings that allegedly use the term "Lord's Day" (see Richard Bauckham, "The Lord's Day," *From Sabbath to Lord's Day: A Biblical, Historical and Theological Investigation*, D.A. Carson, ed. [Grand Rapids, MI: Zondervan, 1982], 223). However, as Ranko Stefanovic points out, "only two of these references, the *Didache* and Ignatius's *To the Magnesians*, are from the early second century, and all others come from the late second century (see Ranko Stefanovic, "The Lord's Day of Revelation 1:10 in the Current Debate," *AUSS* [2011], Vol. 49, No. 2, 263).

30   Translation: Cyril C. Richardson, *Early Christian Fathers* (Louisville, KY: The Westminster Press, 1953), 178.

observance? While many have said yes, not all scholars are convinced. It is possible that this passage does not address a particular day at all. Unlike in Revelation 1:10, the word "day" (*hēmera*) does not appear in the Greek source text.[31] As MacCarty points out, the text "does not supply a noun for the adjective 'Lord's,' leaving the missing noun to be supplied by the translators."[32] In other words, since the text does not provide the noun, translators must ask, "Lord's what?" While "day" seems reasonable, other scholars have offered the word "commandment" or "doctrine" as an alternative.[33] If that is correct, the verse could be translated, "according to the Lord's commandment, come together and break bread and give thanks..."

The support for this alternative option of "commandment" or "doctrine" is that the Greek word (*kata*) at the beginning of the passage, translated "on the," can also be translated "according to," as it is elsewhere in the document.[34] Furthermore, as Bacchiocchi explains, "Didache 14:1 is linked by the conjunction 'and—*de*' to the previous chapter, which closes with the exhortation to 'give according to the commandment' (13:7). The repetition of 'according to—*kata*' could

---

31 See Ranko Stefanovic, "The Lord's Day of Revelation 1:10 in the Current Debate," *AUSS* (2011), Vol. 49, No. 2, 264: "It should be noted here that the text reads κατὰ κυριακὴν δὲ κυρίου. The substantive "day" (ἡμέραν in the accusative case) does not appear in the text, but rather is supplied by the translators and is rendered, "on the Lord's day." However, there is no textual evidence that would warrant such a reading of the text, which is an obvious stretch. Nor does the context indicate that the Lord's day is intended."

32 MacCarty, "The Seventh-Day Sabbath," 36.

33 Bacchiocchi, *From Sabbath to Sunday*, 105; Frank H. Yost, *The Early Christian Sabbath* (Mountain View, CA, 1947), 32: "A number of words, appropriate both grammatically and in meaning, could be supplied...and make as good or better sense than 'day'; for instance, the word 'commandment.'"

34 Didache 1:5; 2:1; 4:13; 6:1, 11; 13:6.

have caused the omission of the word 'commandment' or 'doctrine.'"[35] In other words, the "and" conjunction connects 14:1 to the previous verse, which might indicate that the word "commandment" is implied in 14:1. Moreover, the term "Lord's" (*kuriake*) is used "as an adjective and not as a substantive," indicating that "the issue is not the time but the manner of the celebration of the Lord's Supper."[36] The passage goes on to give prerequisites to the Lord's table—the believers must confess their sins and reconcile with one another. Once again, this indicates that the author addresses not the *time* but the *manner* of the gathering.

However, even if we assume that the author is speaking of a day in Didache 14:1, it is not necessarily the case that he means Sunday. For instance, D. Thomas Lancaster suggests that the Didache's reference to the Lord's day "might have been an uncommon, apostolic way of referring to the Sabbath day."[37] Lancaster cites the *Acts of John* (AD 180), which references the Sabbath as the Lord's day: "on the seventh day, it being the Lord's day."[38] The scholar Aaron Milavec writes, "Given that the Jewish calendar dominates the Didache, the 'divinely instituted

---

35 Bacchiocchi, *From Sabbath to Sunday*, 125, n. 73.

36 Ibid. Bacchiocchi goes on to quote Jean Baptiste Thibaut (*La Liturgie Romaine*, 1924, 33-34): "If it was a question of time, in that case the genius of the Greek language would have simply required the use of the dative: *te kuriake*. The preposition *kata* marks here a relation of conformity. Consequently the word which is implied and to which the qualifying *kuriaken* applies, is not *hemeran* (day) but another term which can be easily supplied, namely the word *didaken* (doctrine) present in the title of the work...The initial phrase of chapter 14...should be translated literally, 'according to the sovereign doctrine of the Lord.'"

37 D. Thomas Lancaster, *Torah Club: Chronicles of the Apostles* (Marshfield, MO: First Fruits of Zion, 2012), 1215.

38 *Acts of John.* Translation: Alexander Walker, Ante-Nicene Fathers, Vol. 8. Edited by Alexander Roberts, James Donaldson, and A. Cleveland Coxe (Buffalo, NY: Christian Literature Publishing Co., 1886).

day' could refer either to the Sabbath or the first day of the week."[39] Since the passage is unclear, the Sabbath seems just as plausible an option as Sunday. Others have suggested that the author is referring to an annual Easter celebration.[40]

Some might argue that the reference to the Lord's Supper suggests that this gathering occurred on a Sunday, but the early Christians did not observe the Lord's Supper on Sunday exclusively. As Bacchiocchi points out, "The New Testament suggests that it was celebrated at *indeterminate* times and on various days (cf. 1 Cor. 11:18, 20, 33, 34)."[41] Indeed, we have evidence of early Christians observing the Lord's Supper *on the Sabbath* in addition to Sunday as late as the fifth century A.D.[42] Additionally, the author urges his readers to "meet together frequently" (16:2), which "hardly suggests exclusive Sunday gatherings."[43]

In summary, there is no noun for the adjective "Lord's" in the Greek source text, meaning that translators must make their best guess as to what is implied in the text. Instead of "day," some scholars suggest "doctrine" or "commandment," which has some textual support.

---

39 Aaron Milavec, *The Didache: Faith, Hope, & Life of the Earliest Christian Communities, 50-70 C.E.* (New York, NY: Newman, 2003), 573.

40 Kenneth Strand, "The 'Lord's Day' in the Second Century," *The Sabbath in Scripture and History*, Kenneth Strand, ed. (Washington: Review and Herald Publishing, 1982), 348. Strand cites C. W. Dugmore, "Lord's Day and Easter," in *Neotestamentica et Patristica* (festschrift for Oscar Cullmann), supplements to *Novum Testamentum* 6 (Leiden, 1962): 272-281.

41 Samuele Bacchiocchi, "The Rise of Sunday Observance in Early Christianity," *The Sabbath in Scripture and History*, Kenneth Strand, ed. (Washington: Review and Herald Publishing, 1982), 133.

42 See Socrates Scholasticus, *Ecclesiastical History* 5.22: "[A]lmost all churches throughout the world celebrate the sacred mysteries on the Sabbath of every week." Quoted in Justo L. González, *A Brief History of Sunday: From the New Testament to the New Creation* (Grand Rapids, MI: Wm. B. Eerdmans Publishing Co., 2017), 58.

43 Bacchiocchi, *From Sabbath to Sunday*, 126, n. 73.

Nevertheless, even if "day" is correct, it is still unclear what the author means by "Lord's day," and it cannot be merely assumed that he means Sunday. Again, some scholars offer alternative suggestions, including the Sabbath or an annual Easter observance. Due to its ambiguity, this passage is unhelpful in clarifying what John meant in Revelation 1:10.

The second writing worthy of comment is Ignatius's *letter to the Magnesians*. Ignatius was a Christian bishop of Antioch. He wrote a series of letters during a trip to Rome, where he was condemned to be executed for his Christian beliefs. His letter to the believers in Magnesia is often cited as an early witness to Sunday observance because of its alleged use of the term "Lord's day." As Richard Lewis writes, Ignatius's testimony "is considered particularly valuable inasmuch as his letters are thought to have been written not later than A.D. 117. Use of the term 'Lord's day' by him would therefore very likely constitute the earliest example of it after Rev 1:10."[44] Here is the relevant passage:

> Those, then, who lived by ancient practices arrived at a new hope. They ceased to keep the Sabbath and lived by the Lord's Day, on which our life as well as theirs shone forth, thanks to him and his death, though some deny this. Through this mystery we got our faith, and because of it we stand our ground so as to become disciples of Jesus Christ, our sole teacher.
> —Ignatius, Magnesians 9:1[45]

A common interpretation of this passage is that Ignatius describes believers who have abandoned Sabbath observance and started observ-

---

44   Richard B. Lewis, "Ignatius and the 'Lord's Day,'" *AUSS* 6.1 (1968), 1.
45   Translation: Richardson, *Early Christian Fathers*, 96.

ing a weekly Lord's day (presumably Sunday) instead. However, a closer look at the passage casts doubts on this interpretation.

For instance, according to Kenneth Strand, "It should be noted that the Greek word for 'day' (*hemeran*, in the accusative case) is not in the text."[46] As with the Didache, "the word 'day' is supplied by the translators, making the phrase read: 'On the Lord's *day*.'"[47] Additionally, as MacCarty points out, "the oldest remaining Greek copy of Ignatius's letter supplies the word 'life' (*zoen*), rendering the phrase, 'living according to the Lord's life.'"[48] It should be noted that Ignatius does not mention the first day of the week anywhere, nor does he say anything about assembling together, worshiping, or resting on any particular day. Ignatius does not seem to be contrasting days as such but rather ways of life more generally.

The surrounding context supports the interpretation that Ignatius is speaking of ways of life instead of days. Elsewhere in the document, Ignatius contrasts living according to Judaism with living according to Christ (Ignatius, *Mag.* 8:1-2; 10:1). Robert Kraft remarks, "It is certainly illegitimate to see behind this context a simple Sabbath/Sunday controversy. It is rather a contrast of two different ways of living—one apart from "grace" ("Judaizing"), the other in the power of the resurrection life."[49] Thus, living according to the Lord's (life) could be understood broadly as living according to Christianity. The phrase "to keep the Sabbath" (to *sabbatize*) here should also be understood as having a broader meaning than merely observing a day.

---

46   Kenneth Strand, "The 'Lord's Day' in the Second Century," *The Sabbath in Scripture and History*, Kenneth Strand, ed. (Washington: Review and Herald Publishing, 1982), 349.

47   Stefanovic, "The Lord's Day of Revelation 1:10," 265.

48   MacCarty, "The Seventh-Day Sabbath," 37.

49   Robert A. Kraft, "Sabbath in Early Christianity," *AUSS* (1965), 28.

Ignatius appears to use this term to mean living according to Judaism. As Herold Weiss explains:

> The verb *to sabbatize* appears in early Christian Greek literature only in Ignatius' *Letter to the Magnesians*, besides the *Gospel of Thomas*. It is clear that Ignatius is contrasting the Jewish with the Christian way of life … It is clear that while Ignatius, unlike Thomas, makes an explicit distinction between Christianity and Judaism, he also uses the verb "to sabbatize" to describe a way of life. For him "To live according to Judaism" (8:1), "to sabbatize" (9:1), and "to judaize" (10:3) are synonymous. He uses these terms interchangeably to advance his argument.[50]

Weiss points out that the verb "to sabbatize" occurs only one other time in early Christian Greek literature: the *Gospel of Thomas*. The author of the *Gospel of Thomas* uses this verb in the same way—not to refer to a specific day but to a way of life that is experienced all the days of the week.[51] Thus, considering the context and the fact that the word "day" does not appear in the text (while the word "life" *does* appear in

---

50   Weiss, *A Day of Gladness*, 210-211.

51   Ibid., 106-107: "For *Thomas* [to sabbatize] means to live in the primordial time of creation week, when God was in motion and at rest. For *Thomas*…the Sabbath is not a sociological marker, not even essentially a commandment, but a reality of the primordial world of the light. Those illumined by the light that shone on the first creation, before the fall, live in a different world all the days of the week. Like God on creation week, they are also characterized by motion and rest at all times. Thomas 27b teaches that in order to see the Father one must "stand at the beginning" and experience God's restful creative motion throughout the week."

the oldest and best manuscripts[52]), the idea that Ignatius is describing weekly Sunday observance seems doubtful.

However, even if we assume that Ignatius is speaking about days, it still is not clear that a weekly Sunday observance is what he means to contrast with the Sabbath. Some scholars have argued that Ignatius refers to an *annual* Sunday observance (Easter).[53] The passage is entirely ambiguous. Even scholars who hold to the traditional view that Ignatius references a weekly Lord's day (Sunday) hesitate to take a firm stand. Richard Bauckham, an advocate for the traditional view, admits that "since the emphasis is on ways of life, we cannot too easily infer that Ignatius must be referring to a *weekly* day of Christian worship to balance the weekly Sabbath...Reference to a weekly Lord's Day would seem more natural, but on the evidence of this text alone we cannot be quite sure."[54] On the other hand (again, assuming Ignatius means to contrast days here), while Ignatius's letter does not give clear evidence

---

52   See Stefanovic, "The Lord's Day of Revelation 1:10: "The statement under consideration comes from the commonly accepted Greek edition of the middle recension of the Ignatian letters. The only surviving Greek manuscript of the middle recension, Codex G (*Codex Mediceus Laurentius*), considered to be the parent of other Greek manuscripts in existence today as well as the Latin translations, actually reads Κατὰ κυριακὴν ζωήν ("according with the Lord's life"). However, the Greek text, reconstructed by modern editors and which serves as the basis for English translations, omits the substantive ζωήν [life] after Κατὰ κυριακὴν [according with the Lord's]. Such a reading bears an obvious impact on the common understanding of the meaning of Κατὰ κυριακὴν [according with the Lord's]. Since the two expressions σαββατίζω and κυριακόν do not occur elsewhere in the Ignatian letters, the readers are left to choose which of the two words, ζωήν [life] (supported by the best manuscripts) or ἡμέραν [day] (as a conjecture), fits the context."

53   Kenneth A. Strand, "Another Look at 'Lord's Day' in the Early Church and in Rev. i. 10," *New Testament Studies*, 13 (1967): 174-182.

54   Richard Bauckham, "The Lord's Day," *From Sabbath to Lord's Day: A Biblical, Historical and Theological Investigation*, D.A. Carson, ed. (Grand Rapids, MI: Zondervan, 1982), 229.

of weekly Sunday observance, this passage *would* seem to imply that Christians were still observing the Sabbath. Some scholars have even argued that Ignatius himself did not oppose Sabbath observance *per se*, but rather a legalistic form of Sabbath observance that was in accordance with certain Jewish teachings that he considered problematic.[55] In any case, if Ignatius refers to a Lord's "day" in this passage, he could just as likely be referring to an *annual* commemoration of the Messiah's resurrection instead of a weekly Sunday observance.

In summary, Ignatius's *letter to the Magnesians* gives no clear indication of early Christian Sunday observance, nor does it provide proof of early use of the term "Lord's day" with reference to Sunday. In the passage we examined, the word "day" does not even appear in the Greek text. The word "life," however, *does* appear in the best manuscripts. Thus, when Ignatius contrasts the Sabbath with the "Lord's (life)," it is more likely that he is contrasting ways of life as opposed to contrasting days. This interpretation is further supported by the context where the author contrasts living in accordance with Judaism with living in accordance with Christ. However, even if Ignatius *does* mean to speak about days specifically, it still is not clear that he refers to weekly Sunday observance. Thus, as with the Didache, this passage from Ignatius is ambiguous and does not help clarify what John meant when he used the term "Lord's day" in Revelation 1:10.

Based on our examination of these early writings, it seems that there is not good evidence that the "Lord's day" in Revelation is referring to Sunday. But what would be the alternative? One popular suggestion is that John was referring to the end-time "Day of the Lord"

---

55 Bacchiocchi, *From Sabbath to Sunday*, 215-217; Lewis, "Ignatius and the 'Lord's Day,'" 45-59; Strand, "The 'Lord's Day' in the Second Century," 348-349; Stefanovic, "The Lord's Day of Revelation 1:10," 261-284.

mentioned throughout Scripture. This does not refer to a singular day but a future period when God will judge the world. Thus, when John said, "I was in the Spirit on the Lord's day," what he likely meant was that the Spirit transported him by way of vision to witness the events that will occur during this period known as the Day of the Lord. This interpretation makes sense in light of the eschatological theme of Revelation and is certainly preferable to the Sunday interpretation.[56] As John Woolvard writes:

> Though today the expression is used commonly of the first day of the week, it is nowhere so used in the Bible…There is no solid evidence, however, that the expression used by John was ever intended to refer to the first day of the week. It is rather a reference to the day of the Lord of the Old Testament, an extended period of time in which God deals in judgment and sovereign rule over the earth. The adjective form can be explained on the ground that in the Old Testament there was no adjectival form for "Lord," and therefore the noun had to be used. The New Testament term is therefore the equivalent to the Old Testament expression "the day of the Lord."[57]

In summary, we have examined three biblical passages that are often cited to support the idea that the earliest Christians observed Sunday. We saw that Acts 20:7 was most likely a special occasion due to Paul leaving the next day, not a weekly meeting. We learned that Paul's instructions in 1 Corinthians 16:2 applied to individual believers or

---

56   For an evaluation of the various interpretations of "Lord's day" in Revelation 1:10, see Stefanovic, "The Lord's Day of Revelation 1:10," 261-284.

57   John Woolvard, *The Revelation of Jesus Christ* (Moody Press, 1966), 42.

households, not a corporate gathering. Finally, upon a close examination of the relevant passages from the Didache and Ignatius's Letter to the Magnesians, we saw that the Sunday interpretation of "Lord's day" in Revelation 1:10 lacks adequate support; a more natural interpretation of the term in Revelation 1:10 is that it refers to the eschatological Day of the Lord. Thus, contrary to what some have claimed, the New Testament evidence does not support a pattern of early Christian Sunday observance.

Sabbath Observance in Early Christianity

Since the Bible does not support replacing Sabbath observance with Sunday observance, how did we get to where we are today, with most Christians not keeping the Sabbath on the seventh day and worshiping on Sunday instead? We will explore that question soon. But first, while the transition from Sabbath to Sunday began early in Christianity, many might be surprised to learn that this change was not immediate, nor was it universal among Christians. For instance, two fifth-century church historians indicate that, well into the fifth century, almost all Christians outside of Alexandria and Rome continued to observe the Sabbath alongside Sunday:

> For although almost all churches throughout the world
> celebrate the sacred mysteries on the Sabbath of every week,
> yet the Christians of Alexandria and at Rome, on account of
> some ancient tradition, have ceased to do this. The Egyptians
> in the neighborhood of Alexandria, and the inhabitants of
> Thebais, hold their religious assemblies on the Sabbath, but

do not participate of the mysteries in the manner usual among Christians in general.[58]

The people of Constantinople, and almost everywhere, assemble together on the Sabbath, as well as on the first day of the week, which custom is never observed in Rome or in Alexandria.[59]

This testimony is significant evidence that demonstrates that "*even as late as the fifth century* almost the entire Christian world observed *both Saturday and Sunday* for special religious services."[60] Indeed, according to the historical evidence, the early Christians did not consider Sunday a replacement for the Sabbath at this time.[61] Again, outside of Alexandria and Rome, most Christians observed both days.

Additionally, in the fourth-century *Apostolic Constitutions*, a collection of eight Christian treatises, there are "a number of prescriptions relating to the Sabbath as well as Sunday."[62] For example, in the name of Peter and Paul, the following instruction is given:

---

58   Socrates Scholasticus, *Ecclesiastical History* 5.22. Quoted in González, A Brief History of Sunday, 58.

59   Sozomen, *Ecclesiastical History* 7.19. Quoted in González, A Brief History of Sunday, 58.

60   Kenneth A. Strand, "The Sabbath and Sunday From the Second Through Fifth Centuries," *The Sabbath in Scripture and History* (Washington, D.C.: Review and Herald Publishing., 1982), 324.

61   See Justo L. González, *A Brief History of Sunday*, 39: "[T]he linking of the fourth commandment with Sunday observances, which would later become commonplace in Christian piety and theology, is notably absent from the ancient church."

62   Strand, "The Sabbath and Sunday From the Second Through Fifth Centuries," 324. Strand cites *Apostolic Constitutions* 7:413, 7:469, 7:474, 7:417, and 7:495.

Slaves are to work five days. But on the Sabbath and the Lord's Day they are to have freedom to attend church in order to receive religious instruction. We [Peter and Paul] have ordered this for the Sabbath because of creation; and for the Lord's day because of the resurrection.

—Apostolic Constitutions 8.33[63]

Another example of Christian Sabbath observance comes from the fourth-century historian, Epiphanius, who records that the sect of Jewish Christians known as the Nazarenes still observed the Sabbath in his time.[64] According to Ray Pritz, these Nazarenes were isolated from Judaism because of their allegiance to Yeshua the Messiah. They were also later rejected by Christianity because they "continued to observe certain aspects of Mosaic Law, including circumcision and the Sabbath."[65] However, apparently the Nazarenes' exclusion from Christianity was gradual. According to Pritz, they "were not included in the earlier heresy lists because they were simply not considered heretical

---

63 Quoted in González, *A Brief History of Sunday*, 54.

64 See Epiphanius, *Adversus Haereses* 29.7.1-5: "The Nazarenes do not differ in any essential thing from them [i.e. Jews], since they practice the custom and doctrines prescribed by the Jewish law, except that they believe in Christ. They believe in the resurrection of the dead and that the universe was created by God. They preach that God is one and that Jesus Christ is his Son. They are very learned in the Hebrew language. They read the law ... Therefore they differ both from the Jews and from the Christians; from the former, because they believe in Christ; from the true Christians because they fulfill till now Jewish rites as the circumcision, the Sabbath and others." (Quoted in Bacchiocchi, *From Sabbath to Sunday*, 147.)

65 Ray A. Pritz, *Nazarene Jewish Christianity: From the End of the New Testament Period Until Its Disappearance in the Fourth Century* (The Hebrew University, Jerusalem: The Magnes Press, 1988), 109.

enough or a threat to 'orthodoxy.'"[66] In any case, the Nazarenes give us further evidence of continued Christian Sabbath observance as late as the fourth century.

Moreover, a "longer version" of Ignatius's letter to the Magnesians, produced by an unknown interpolator in the fourth century, admonishes Christians to observe *both* the Sabbath and the "Lord's day" (Sunday).[67] According to historian Justo L. González, "This interpolation shows that, at least as late as the fourth century, some or perhaps even most Christians observed the Sabbath, and then the Lord's day on the following day. In other words, the Lord's day, celebrated on the first day of the week, was not a substitution for the Sabbath, but a separate celebration of the resurrection of Jesus."[68]

Throughout history, there has always been a faithful minority of Christians who continued to observe the Sabbath on the seventh day. Numerous historical sources, all the way through the Reformation to modern times, testify to this fact.[69] Many of these Christians observed both the Sabbath and Sunday. Nevertheless, most Christians today observe only Sunday, and many of them see Sunday as the "Christian Sabbath" that has replaced the biblical Sabbath. How did this happen?

---

66 Ibid.

67 See Pseudo-Ignatius, *Magnesians* 9:3-4: "Let us therefore no longer keep the Sabbath after the Jewish manner, and rejoice in days of idleness...But let everyone of you keep the Sabbath after a special manner, rejoicing in the meditation of the law, admiring the workmanship of God...And after the observance of the Sabbath, let every friend of Christ keep the Lord's Day as a festival, the resurrection-day, the queen and chief of all the days" (Quoted in González, *A Brief History of Sunday*, 22).

68 González, *A Brief History of Sunday*, 23.

69 See González, *A Brief History of Sunday*; Strand, *The Sabbath in Scripture and History*.

A Shift from Sabbath to Sunday

The earliest clear evidence of Christian Sunday observance appears in the second century AD. The *Epistle of Barnabas* (135 AD), which was written in Alexandria, references a weekly "eighth day" (which is also the first day, Sunday) celebration. The author of this epistle denigrates Sabbath observance as something "impossible" for humans to fulfill (*Barnabas* 15:6) and advocates observing Sunday instead, "for this is the day that Jesus rose from among the dead" (*Barnabas* 15:9).[70] The author of this epistle "lived at the crucial time when Emperor Hadrian (117-138 C.E.) adopted rigorous and repressive measures against the Jews, outlawing their religious observances and particularly their Sabbath-keeping."[71] This conflict between the Jews and the empire "made it necessary for Christians to develop a new identity in order to avoid the repressive and punitive measures (fiscal, military, political, and literary) aimed at the Jews."[72]

Decades later (150 AD), Justin Martyr of Rome also references Sunday observance as a celebration of the Messiah's resurrection (*First Apology*, 67). Additionally, in his other writings, he expresses a negative attitude toward the Sabbath and Jews. For instance, Justin argues that God gave the Sabbath to Jews only because of their transgressions and hard hearts (*Dialogue with Trypho* 18).

It appears that the abandoning of Sabbath observance and adoption of exclusive Sunday observance emerged first in Alexandria and Rome and was largely motived by an anti-Jewish sentiment.[73] But once

---

70   Quoted in González, *A Brief History of Sunday*, 29.

71   Geraty, "From Sabbath to Sunday: Why, How and When?" 266.

72   Ibid., 266-267.

73   See MacCarty, "The Seventh-Day Sabbath," 42: "Anti-Jewish sentiment led some church leaders to disparage keeping the Sabbath of the Ten Commandments, to help separate Christianity from Judaism."

again, these motivations were not universal.[74] As we examined earlier, many Christians living outside of Alexandria and Rome continued to observe the Sabbath in addition to Sunday as late as the fifth century. Kenneth Strand gives an excellent summary of what the historical sources indicate:

> It has become obvious that the displacement of Saturday by
> Sunday as a day of weekly Christian worship and rest was a
> long and slow process. Until the second century there is no
> concrete evidence of a Christian *weekly* Sunday celebration
> anywhere. The first specific references during that century
> come from Alexandria and Rome, places that also early
> rejected observance of the seventh-day Sabbath. In this early
> substitution of Sunday for Saturday, however, the Christian
> churches in Alexandria and Rome were unique. Evidence from
> the fifth century indicates that also at that time *both Sabbath*
> *and Sunday* were observed generally throughout the Christian
> world—except in Rome and Alexandra.[75]

Much more could be said about the political and social influences that brought about the decline of Sabbath observance and the rise of

---

74   See Bruce M. Metzger, *Studies in Lectionary Text of the Greek New Testament* (Chicago, IL: University of Chicago Press, 1944), vol. 2, sec. 3, p. 12: "The difference between East and West in the observance of the Sabbath can be accounted for by a reasonable historical explanation. In the West, particularly after the Jewish rebellion under Hadrian, it became vitally important for those who were not Jews to avoid exposing themselves to suspicion; and the observance of the Sabbath was one of the most noticeable indications of Judaism. In the East, however, less opposition was shown to Jewish institutions."

75   Strand, "The Sabbath and Sunday From the Second Through Fifth Centuries," 330.

Sunday observance in early Christianity.[76] Still, one thing is clear: the earliest Christians did not consider Sunday a replacement of the Sabbath. While most Christians did come to observe Sunday, many continued to observe the Sabbath as well. As Justo González writes, "While Christians gathered on the first day of the week to break bread and to celebrate baptisms, many of them—certainly Jewish Christians, but probably most others—continued viewing the seventh day with great reverence, probably seeking to rest as much as the social order to which they were subjected allowed."[77] Moreover, Sunday was not originally a day of rest. According to Strand, "when the Christian weekly Sunday first emerged, it continued to be a day of work, although it included a worship service in honor of Christ's resurrection."[78]

So, how did Sunday eventually become recognized as the "Christian Sabbath"? Well, on March 7, 321 AD, the long process of Sunday taking on the characteristics of the Sabbath and replacing the seventh day as the Sabbath was initiated. On this date, the emperor Constantine decreed that Sunday would be a day of rest. His edict said:

> On the venerable day of the Sun let the magistrates and people residing in cities rest, and let all workshops be closed. In the country however persons engaged in agriculture may freely and lawfully continue their pursuits because it often happens that another day is not suitable for grain-sowing or vine planting; lest by neglecting the proper moment for such operations the

---

76 See Bacchiocchi, *From Sabbath to Sunday*; Geraty, "From Sabbath to Sunday," 255-268.

77 González, *A Brief History of Sunday*, 131.

78 Strand, "The Sabbath and Sunday From the Second Through Fifth Centuries," 330.

bounty of heaven should be lost.

—Codex Justinianus 3.12.3[79]

Constantine's edict made Sunday "a state-legislated day of rest throughout the Roman Empire."[80] González summarizes the significance that this edict had for Christians:

> Now that Sunday became a day of rest, civil laws had to
> determine what work was lawful on that day. This was soon
> followed by ecclesiastical laws, also determining which
> activities were allowed on Sunday, and which were forbidden.
> Under such circumstances, it is not surprising that Sunday was
> now connected with Sabbath rest and with the commandment
> ordering it. This was the great change introduced by Constantine's decree. It brought about a connection between Sunday
> and Sabbath rest that was not present in earlier Christian
> thought and devotion. In the long run, this would lead to discussions as to whether Sunday abolished the Sabbath, whether
> Christian worship should be on the Sabbath, and so on.[81]

Constantine's decree opened the door for later ecclesiastical authorities to discourage Sabbath observance and mandate Sunday observance exclusively. For instance, around sixty years after Constantine's edict, the Council of Laodicea's Canon 29 demanded, "Christians must not

---

79 Translated in Philip Schaff, *History of the Christian Church* (New York: Thomas Y. Crowell, 1894), 1:487.

80 MacCarty, "The Seventh-Day Sabbath," 43.

81 González, *A Brief History of Sunday*, 45.

Judaize by resting on the Sabbath, but must work on that day, rather honoring the Lord's Day; and, if they can, resting then as Christians."[82]

As time went on, church authorities increasingly disparaged Sabbath observance and promoted only Sunday observance.[83] As Strand remarks, "This process brought about a widespread conflict of Sunday with the seventh-day Sabbath, and eventually in medieval times this Sunday 'Sabbath' came to displace the original Saturday Sabbath generally throughout Europe."[84] Indeed, after the Reformation, in English-speaking countries, Sunday not only replaced the Sabbath but also even came to be called the Sabbath.[85] Protestant Christian confessions (such as the Westminster Confession, quoted at the beginning of this chapter), sermons, and literature all affirm the Sabbath commandment, yet Sunday is what is meant. The Sabbath was changed from

---

82 Council of Laodicea's Canon 29. Quoted in D. Thomas Lancaster, *From Sabbath to Sabbath: Returning the Holy Sabbath to the Disciples of Jesus* (Marshfield, MO: First Fruits of Zion, 2016), 269.

83 See MacCarty, "The Seventh-Day Sabbath," 43: "Pope Innocent I, in an early fifth-century decretal attempting further to discourage seventh-day Sabbath observance, declared, "In these two days [Friday and Saturday] one should not celebrate the sacraments." Leo I issued another Sunday law in 469. In 534 Emperor Justinian revised the Roman law code, incorporating the previous official Sunday laws of Constantine and Leo I. The Council of Orleans in 538 prohibited labor, even for farmers, so they could attend worship services on Sunday. With these decrees the Sabbath commandment had been completely reversed, turning the Sabbath into a common workday and Sunday into a day of rest."

84 Kenneth A. Strand, "The Sabbath and Sunday From the Second Through Fifth Centuries," 330.

85 See González, *A Brief History of Sunday*, 152-153: "[A]lthough there had long been a tendency to connect Sunday with the fourth commandment, it was mostly after the Reformation, and particularly in the English-speaking world, that the word "Sabbath" came to mean Sunday. This was not possible in romance languages, where various derivatives from 'Sabbath' were still the name of the seventh day of the week. Thus it was mostly in English-speaking countries that Sabbatarianism developed, in the sense of calling Sunday the Sabbath."

Saturday to Sunday not by the Scriptures, but by political edicts and church councils centuries after the time of the apostles.

Conclusion

In this chapter, we saw how the New Testament demonstrates that the earliest Christians continued to keep the Sabbath in accordance with the biblical commandment. The New Testament references to the first day of the week do not establish weekly Sunday meetings and certainly do not support a replacement of the Sabbath with Sunday. Christians in the early centuries after the time of the apostles did not universally reject Sabbath observance; most Christians observed both the Sabbath and Sunday as late as the fifth century. The decline of Sabbath observance and the rise of exclusive Sunday observance in early Christianity emerged first in Alexandria and Rome and was largely motived by anti-Jewish sentiment. Nevertheless, Sunday was not considered a day of rest until 321 A.D., when Constantine decreed that Sunday be a day of rest. This edict started the long process of Christians assigning to Sunday the characteristics of the Sabbath commandment. However, Scripture nowhere endorses this change.

CHAPTER 4

ANSWERING OBJECTIONS: THE SABBATH IS ONLY FOR JEWS

A person might concede that the Sabbath was never abolished or changed but still argue that it is applicable only to Jewish believers. For instance, D. Thomas Lancaster argues that while Gentile believers are welcome to observe the Sabbath if they like, "God did not make the observance of the Sabbath into a universal commandment that is binding upon all human beings or even into a commandment that is binding upon all believers. Instead he gave the privilege of being obligated to keep the Sabbath only to one people, his people Israel."[1] Lancaster goes on to state, "For Gentile believers, Sabbath observance is optional."[2]

Does God have a different standard for Jewish believers than he does for Gentile believers? Are Gentile believers exempt from obedience to the Sabbath commandment? No. The New Testament clearly indicates that the Sabbath applies to Gentile and Jewish believers alike.

First, as we saw in chapter 1, in Matthew 5:17-20, Yeshua affirmed the enduring validity and authority of the Torah, and the Torah includes the command to observe the Sabbath. He admonished his followers to do and teach even the least of the Torah's commandments

---

1   D. Thomas Lancaster, *From Sabbath to Sabbath: Returning the Holy Sabbath to the Disciples of Jesus* (Marshfield, MO: First Fruits of Zion, 2016), 56.

2   Ibid., 72.

(and the Sabbath is far from the "least" of the commandments). Later, in Matthew 28:19-20, he instructs his disciples to teach the Gentiles to observe "all" that he commanded them. Since Yeshua commanded his disciples to observe even the least of the Torah's commandments, it follows that he expected his disciples to teach the Gentiles to observe even the least of the Torah's commandments. This means that the Gentile believers would have been taught to observe the Sabbath.

Second, in Mark 2:27, Yeshua says that the Sabbath was "made for man." That is, God established the Sabbath in creation for all mankind, not just the Jewish people (Genesis 2:2-3). As Roy Gane puts it, "It is clear that God instituted the Sabbath for all human beings on planet Earth because He instituted it in the beginning, long before Israel existed, along with basic elements of human life such as marriage and labor."[3] Indeed, marriage was also instituted for man's benefit at creation. Nobody believes that marriage is an exclusively Jewish institution—God established it to bless all mankind, just like he did the Sabbath.

Third, writing to Gentiles,[4] the apostle Peter says, "As obedient children, do not be conformed to the passions of your former ignorance, but as he who called you is holy, you also be holy in all your conduct, since it is written, 'You shall be holy, for I am holy'" (1 Peter 1:14-16). The phrase, "You shall be holy, for I am holy," comes from Leviticus 19:2. The very next verse, Leviticus 19:3, says "you shall keep my Sabbaths."

The New Testament's teaching that the Sabbath commandment applies to both Jewish and Gentile believers isn't surprising considering

---

3   Roy Gane, "Sabbath and the New Covenant," *JATS*, 10/1-2 (1999), 316.

4   Peter's description of his readers' former life as one of ignorance and futility inherited from their forefathers (1:14, 18) indicates people who were not from a Jewish background.

what the Old Testament says. The fourth commandment itself specifies that Sabbath rest is expected of not only Israel but also "the sojourner," that is, non-native Israelites who have embraced Israel's God (Exodus 20:10). Isaiah 56:3-8 specifically references "the foreigner who has joined himself to the Lord." Isaiah describes these foreigners as ones who keep the Sabbath and hold fast to the covenant. God is so pleased with these Gentiles' Sabbath observance that he promises them an "everlasting name that shall not be cut off" and welcomes them in his "house of prayer for all peoples" (Isaiah 56:5-7).

God did not intend for Israel to keep the Torah to themselves; he intended for them to share it with the nations, so that they would see the wisdom and value of God's laws (Deuteronomy 4:5-8). Indeed, God's desire has always been that the Gentiles would come to faith and embrace his ways, including the Sabbath. This desire is clearly expressed in Isaiah's prophecy that eventually all mankind will observe the Sabbath in the world to come (Isaiah 66:23).

Acts 15 — The Jerusalem Council

Despite these clear passages in the Old and New Testament that affirm Sabbath observance for both Jewish and Gentile believers, some argue that Acts 15 proves that Gentile believers were freed from having to observe commandments such as the Sabbath. As John MacArthur states, "the Jerusalem council did not impose Sabbath keeping on the Gentile believers."[5] But did the Jerusalem council really conclude that Gentiles do not need to observe the Sabbath? Not at all. When we examine Acts 15 closely, we discover that this passage was not about whether or not Gentile believers should observe commands like the Sabbath. Instead, the issue confronting the Jerusalem council was

---

5   John MacArthur, "Is the Sabbath for Today?" *Grace to You.* www.gty.org.

whether or not Gentiles must convert to Judaism in order to be "saved" and received among God's people. The opening verses make this clear:

> But some men came down from Judea and were teaching the brothers, "Unless you are circumcised according to the custom of Moses, you cannot be saved." And after Paul and Barnabas had no small dissension and debate with them, Paul and Barnabas and some of the others were appointed to go up to Jerusalem to the apostles and the elders about this question.
> —Acts 15:1-2

Here we see that certain Jews insisted that the only way Gentiles could be "saved" was to become Jewish through ritual conversion.[6] During the Hasmonean period (140-37 BC), circumcision began to be associated with conversion to Judaism.[7] By the first century,

---

6   See Terence L. Donaldson, *Paul and the Gentiles: Remapping the Apostle's Convictional World* (Minneapolis: Fortress Press, 2006), 275: "[O]ne can identify a strand within Judaism holding to the rigorous position that only those Gentiles who became proselytes in this age would be granted a share in salvation in the age to come. The presence of this strand in Tannaitic material (t.Sanh. 13.2; b.'Abod. Zar. 3b; b.Yeb. 24b; Pesiq. R. 161a) suggests the likelihood that it was present among the Pharisees as well."

7   See Shaye J. D. Cohen, *The beginnings of Jewishness: Boundaries, Varieties, Uncertainties* (Los Angeles: University of California Press, 1999), 136, 169: "The Hasmonean period witnesses for the first time in the history of Judaism the establishment of processes by which outsiders can become insiders, non-Judaeans can become Judaeans, and non-Jews can become Jews...What must a gentile do in order to achieve social integration into the Jewish community? The only empirical or 'objective' requirement that our sources reveal is circumcision for men. Circumcision can signal either theological conversion (cf. Achior in Judith)—that is, acceptance or belief in the God of the Jews—or commitment to observe the Jewish laws (as in Josephus, for whom 'to be circumcised' and 'to adopt the customs of the Jews' are synonymous), or the assumption of membership or citizenship within the community (as in the case of the Idumaeans and Ituraeans). No matter

circumcision was synonymous with Jewish identity.[8] This is the historical backdrop of the Jerusalem council debate. This controversy over
whether a Gentile must become circumcised—that is, become Jewish
via ritual conversion—as a prerequisite to salvation is the same issue
Paul addresses in Galatians. As Tim Hegg explains:

> [T]he term "circumcision" is used as a shorthand way of
> describing proselytism—that rabbinic ceremony by which a
> Gentile person would be given the status of being a Jew and
> therefore qualify to have a place in the world to come [m.San-
> hedrin 10.1]. Given this understanding, one is in a far better
> position to understand why Paul speaks so strongly against
> circumcision (Gal 5:2-3). He is not arguing against the biblical
> commandments, as is seen by the fact that he has Timothy
> circumcised (Acts 16:1f). In Galatians, Paul is using "circum-
> cision" to mean "to become a proselyte," that is, to accept the

---

what its import, circumcision was essential; without it social conversion for men was
impossible."

8   See James Dunn, *The New Perspective on Paul* (Eerdmans, 2008), 315: "The basic point
is that circumcision was inextricably bound up with Jewish identity, that is, with the
identity of the Jews as the people of Israel, the people chosen by God from among all
the other nations to be his own." See also Tim Hegg, *Why We Keep Torah: Ten Persistent
Questions* (Tacoma, WA: TorahResource, 2009), 91: "In the 1st Century, circumcision was
no longer simply the sign of the covenant with Abraham—it had long since combined
with a cultural imperative to define Jewishness (at least as far as males were concerned).
So clearly had circumcision become an ideological identity marker for Jews, that Paul
could utilize the term 'the circumcision' to mean 'Jewish people' [e.g., Romans 4:12;
15:8]. This was also the standard perspective of pagan authors. For them, 'circumcision'
and 'Jewish' were one and the same."

idea that "becoming a Jew" would secure a place in the world to come.[9]

Again, the question in Acts 15 was not over whether the Gentile believers should be exempted from observing laws like the Sabbath. The question was, must the Gentile believers in Messiah convert to Judaism to be saved? To put it another way, could only Jews (whether by means of ethnicity or conversion) be saved? The Jews pressuring the Gentile believers to get circumcised in Acts 15 said yes. They believed that salvation was available only to Jews and that conversion (a ritual process culminating with circumcision) was how Gentiles could be incorporated into the Jewish people.[10]

---

9   Tim Hegg, *Why We Keep Torah: Ten Persistent Questions* (Tacoma, WA: TorahResource, 2009), 129.

10   See Caleb Hegg, *Instruction for Community, Family, & Personal Living: A Commentary on Colossians & Philemon* (Growing in Messiah, 2021), 57-58: "A belief that circumcision changed a person's ethnic status is also put forward by Josephus who relates a story, set during Paul's lifetime, of a Parthian prince and eventual king, who takes upon himself the commands of Torah. This prince, named Izates, wants to complete his devotion to the Lord by becoming circumcised but his mother advises against it. Izates is able to live out the Torah without consequence, but taking on the final step of circumcision would place him in a different category. It would define him as a 'Jew' in the eyes of his people [Josephus, Antiquities. 20.38-39]. Izates was originally taught about God and the laws of Torah by a Jew named Ananias. When Izates was considering circumcision he told Ananias what his mother had said and the advisor agreed with his mother [Antiquities 20.41]. Josephus then introduces another advisor to Izates, a Jew named Eleazer who is described as being 'esteemed very skillful in the learning of his country' (20.43). Eleazer has a different understanding than Ananias and believes that Izates should become circumcised [Antiquities 20.44-45]. Izates ends up calling for a physician and becomes circumcised. We can first note that 'Judaism' within the first century was not monolithic. We have two Jews with two very different views. One believes Izates should keep the Torah and the customs but not undergo the final step of circumcision. While the other view believes keeping the Torah and customs without being circumcised is

The apostles had a different perspective, which was based on Scripture instead of man-made conversion formulas. They believed that Jews and Gentiles are saved "through the grace of the Lord Jesus" (Acts 15:11), not by being circumcised or being sufficiently Jewish. (After all, as Paul argues in Romans 4, Abraham himself was justified by faith long before God commanded him to be circumcised.) Peter saw Gentiles receiving the Spirit and being saved with his own eyes (Acts 15:7-8), and James recognized that this was a fulfillment of prophetic texts that declared that Gentiles would seek the Lord (Acts 15:13-18; cf. Amos 9:11-12). Thus, the apostles determined that requiring Gentile believers to convert to Judaism to be saved was a burdensome yoke that shouldn't be placed upon them (Acts 15:10). After all, not even Jewish believers could be saved apart from grace.[11] As J. K. McKee explains:

> The yoke being placed upon these non-Jewish Believers in the Messiah was a legalistic perversion of the Torah which demanded that if you do not observe it and convert to Judaism (perhaps according to the particular sect represented) you cannot be saved. It is a yoke that keeps people *out* of God's intention, rather than one that welcomes them *in*. It is making

---

against the very Torah Izates is attempting to keep. We should also highlight the fact that circumcision is the final step in 'conversion.' Izates is not considered a Jew even when he follows the commands of Torah and the customs of the Jews. In other words, this king can live and worship according to the Torah and the customs of the Jews all he wants, but no one considers him Jewish or part of the covenant people until he undergoes the act of circumcision. This one ritual act changes everything and places the king in a totally different category, not only for the Jews, but for the Gentiles under his rule."

11 See Craig Keener, *Acts* (Cambridge University Press, 2020), 366: "The law is good, but even Jewish believers did not meet its standard without grace (Acts 15:10-11); seeking to be justified by divine instruction abused its purpose. Judean believers thus dare not lay on others a burden they could not lift themselves (Luke 11:46)."

people from the nations into ethnic Jews in order for them
to be a part of God's own, when faith in God (and now His
Messiah) has always been the primary focus of being identified
as His own (Genesis 15:6).[12]

After considering all the arguments, James stood up and proclaimed, "we should not trouble those of the Gentiles who turn to
God" (Acts 15:19). That is, the Gentiles were not to be pressured into
converting to Judaism and taking on the entire Torah all at once (contra
the Pharisees in Acts 15:5). Instead, they were to be received as members of the believing community because of their faith in the Messiah.
Nevertheless, there was still a need to assure the Jewish community
that these Gentiles were sincere in their commitment to follow the
God of Israel. Therefore, James proclaimed that the Gentile believers
were to start with four basic rules from the Torah[13] to show that they
had fully renounced idolatry and embraced the God of Israel (Acts
15:20). These four rules directly relate to rejecting idolatrous worship
practices.[14] Obviously, these four rules were not a comprehensive list

---

12   J. K. McKee, *Acts 15 for the Practical Messianic* (McKinney, TX: Messianic Apologetics,
      2010), 53.

13   Exodus 34:15; Leviticus 17:13-16; 18; 20:6-21; Numbers 25:1-2; Deuteronomy 12:16, 23.
      The "what has been strangled" is likely prohibited on the basis of the Torah's ban on
      eating blood. Philo criticizes pagans for strangling their sacrifices and not letting the
      blood drain out (*Special Laws* 4.122).

14   See Ben Witherington III, *The Acts of the Apostles: A Socio-Rhetorical Commentary*
      (Grand Rapids, MI: Eerdmans, 1998), 463: "They must not give Jews in the Diaspora
      the opportunity to complain that Gentile Christians were still practicing idolatry and
      immorality by going to pagan feasts even after beginning to follow Christ." See also Tim
      Hegg, *An Assessment of the "Divine Invitation" Teaching* (Tacoma, WA: TorahResource,
      2009), 40: "The most adequate explanation for the Four Prohibitions is that they prohibit
      common practices associated with the pagan temples and were therefore understood as

of laws defining Gentile Christian morality but a starting point of fellowship. Since this list was not intended to define the full expression of Gentile obedience, the Sabbath's absence from the list implies nothing in regard to whether Gentiles should observe it. Furthermore, the Gentile believers were expected to attend the synagogue services every Sabbath to be instructed in Moses's teaching: "For from ancient generations Moses has had in every city those who proclaim him, for he is read every Sabbath in the synagogues" (Acts 15:21). As we can see, far from exempting Gentiles from Sabbath observance, Acts 15:21 assumes that these Gentile believers would be observing the Sabbath alongside Jewish believers.[15]

---

such (without further explanation), since Gentiles with a history in the pagan temples would immediately recognize the association. So the primary purpose of the Four Prohibitions was to assure the believing Jewish community that the believing Gentiles had made a clear and permanent break with their former idolatrous practices."

15   Some have suggested that the reiteration of the Apostolic decree in Acts 21:25 is a contrasting remark to Paul's need to demonstrate his commitment to the Torah in Acts 21:23-24. In other words, while Paul must prove his loyalty to the Torah, Gentile believers need only to keep the four requirements. But the text does not support this view. See J. K. McKee, *Acts 15 for the Practical Messianic* (McKinney, TX: Messianic Apologetics, 2010), 191-192: "Many Bibles begin v. 25 as 'But concerning/as...' (NASU, RSV, NKJV, NRSV, ESV), which serves to support this as a contrasting statement to Paul's Jewish loyalty. However, the opening preposition and conjunction, *peri de*, can be rendered as 'And concerning/as...' (YLT, LITV), with no real contrast to be implied... Vs. 22-25 taken together are to serve that Paul is a Jew loyal to the Torah, and is no apostate. Paul, by going through the purification ritual, will prove this to be true, and James' repetition of the Apostolic decree will additionally show that the claims against him are to be considered false...The placement of v. 25 within James' and the Jerusalem leaders' discussion with Paul does not at all need to be taken as meaning that the non-Jewish Believers were not required to progress beyond the four prohibitions...Vs. 22-25 are used to remind the reader that the Apostle Paul is a man who is 'orderly, keeping the Law' because 'concerning the Gentiles who have believed, we wrote...', which Paul at the Jerusalem Council agreed to. Paul's implementation of the Apostolic decree among

In summary, the issue in dispute in Acts 15 was whether or not Gentiles must convert to Judaism in order to be "saved" and received among God's people. The apostles declared that the Gentile believers are not required to convert to Judaism and that both Jews and Gentiles are saved by grace through faith. James ruled that the Gentiles needed to keep four Torah requirements, not as the full expression of their obedience as believers, but as the starting point of fellowship to demonstrate to the Jewish community that they had renounced pagan idolatry and were sincere in their commitment to the God of Israel. This controversy had nothing to do with whether or not Gentile believers were exempt from keeping the Sabbath or any other commandments. In fact, the conclusion of the Jerusalem council assumes that Gentiles would be attending synagogue services every Sabbath to learn the Torah alongside Jewish believers.

Was the Sabbath an Old Covenant institution given only to Israel?

Another argument against Sabbath observance for Gentile believers is that the Sabbath was part of a covenant that is now obsolete. The Sabbath was part of the "Old Covenant" that God made with Israel at Sinai. The New Covenant that was inaugurated by the Messiah's work on the cross does not require Sabbath observance. Therefore, in the "New Covenant era," the Sabbath does not apply anymore—especially not to Gentile believers. As John MacArthur asserts, "The Sabbath was the sign to Israel of the Old Covenant (Ex 31:16-17; Neh. 9:14; Ezek.

---

the nations confirms his obedience to the Torah, that he is not rogue and completely independent from Jerusalem, and that the introduction of non-Jews is not tantamount to introducing Greco-Roman paganism into the *ekklesia*!"

20:12). Because we are now under the New Covenant (Heb. 8), we are no longer required to keep the sign of the Old Covenant."[16]

Is this conclusion in line with Scripture? If we examine this issue further, we will discover several problems with this reasoning. First, Yeshua said that the Sabbath was made for mankind (Mark 2:27). When was the Sabbath made? It was established at creation (Genesis 2:3), long before there even was an Israel. At the very beginning, before any "Old Covenant," God gave the Sabbath to all mankind for our benefit.

Now, one could argue that while the Sabbath was established at creation, there is no reference to people *actually observing* the Sabbath until Moses. As MacArthur states, "There is no evidence of anyone's keeping the Sabbath before the time of Moses, nor are there any commands to keep the Sabbath before the giving of the law at Mount Sinai."[17] However, the lack of an explicit reference to people observing the Sabbath before Moses is irrelevant. As Ronald Dart explains, "The book of Genesis is not a book of laws but a book of history. The Sabbath played no special role in that history. References to the law in Genesis are incidental."[18] For instance, we know from Genesis that adultery and lying are sins because of the incidents in the Genesis narratives that revealed the existence of God's expectations in these areas (e.g., Genesis 20:1-9). But these expectations are not explicitly stated as commandments until Moses's time. That doesn't mean that adultery and lying were any less a violation of God's standards. Similarly, the mention of the Sabbath in the creation account illustrates God's expec-

---

16   John MacArthur, "Is the Sabbath for Today?" *Grace to You.* www.gty.org.

17   Ibid.

18   Ronald L. Dart, "Examining arguments for and against the Sabbath," *ProTorah.* www. protorah.com.

tation that his people keep it. God didn't rest on the Sabbath because he was tired; he rested on the Sabbath as an example for his people to follow (Genesis 2:2; Exodus 20:11). Craig Keener puts this point well:

> As I tried to study the biblical text honestly, I could see that this was not just a matter of keeping laws designated for Israel; God actually modeled the Sabbath rest in creation (Gen 2:2-3). Whether we take that narrative literally or not, the principle of the Sabbath is there, and it apparently is an example for all people, not just those who are ethnically descended from Abraham.[19]

The second problem with the argument that the Sabbath doesn't apply to Gentile believers because it is part of the "Old Covenant" between God and Israel is that the New Covenant is *also* between God and Israel: "Behold, the days are coming, declares the Lord, when I will make a new covenant with the house of Israel and the house of Judah" (Jeremiah 31:31; cf. Hebrews 8:8). So, if we say that the Sabbath doesn't apply to Gentile believers because it was a covenant sign between God and Israel alone, then by that same logic, the *New Covenant* does not apply to Gentile believers either. In reality, "Israel" has always included those of the nations who draw near to God in faith. In the book of Ephesians, we clearly see that Gentiles who are "brought near by the blood of Christ" are no longer "strangers to the covenants of promise" but are incorporated into "the commonwealth of Israel" and become "fellow citizens with the saints and members of the household of God" (Ephesians 2:11-22). While it is true that the Sabbath was a sign of

---

19   Craig Keener, "Which day is the Sabbath?" *Bible Background: Research and Commentary from Dr. Craig Keener.* www.craigkeener.com.

the covenant between God and Israel, it is also true that Gentiles in Messiah are members of the commonwealth of Israel. Therefore, the Sabbath is for Gentile believers too.

The third problem with appealing to the New Covenant to dismiss the Sabbath is that the New Covenant affirms Sabbath observance. One of the promises of the New Covenant is that God will write his Torah, his law, on the hearts of his people:

> For this is the covenant that I will make with the house of Israel after those days, declares the Lord: I will put my law within them, and I will write it on their hearts. And I will be their God, and they shall be my people.
> —Jeremiah 31:33 (cf. Hebrews 8:10)

Members of the New Covenant will have God's Torah inscribed upon their hearts, producing obedience to the commandments. This is what Ezekiel describes when he proclaims that God will give his people a new heart, put his Spirit within them, and cause them "to walk in my statutes and be careful to obey my rules" (Ezekiel 36:27). Paul alludes to these prophecies when he characterizes believers as those who live out "the righteous requirement of the law" because they walk "according to the Spirit" (Romans 8:4). And once again, this promise does not just apply to Jewish believers. Gentile believers are given the same Spirit in accordance with the New Covenant promise (Acts 15:8). Of course, this law that God writes upon his people's hearts includes the Sabbath.

Some might object and say that this promise does not include laws like the Sabbath because the New Covenant is "not like" the covenant made at Sinai (Jeremiah 31:32). But Jeremiah did not say that the Torah would be different in the New Covenant. What is different in the New Covenant is the people's *response* to the Torah. Indeed, the problem was that Israel was not faithful to the covenant: "For they did not continue in my covenant" (Hebrews 8:9; cf. Jeremiah 31:32). The New Covenant is different because God will put his Torah on his people's hearts, generating the proper response. Unlike the previous generation, members of the New Covenant *will* be faithful to the Torah. We have no reason to think that the Torah that God writes on the hearts of his people in the New Covenant is different from the Torah he wanted to be on his people's hearts all along (e.g., Deuteronomy 6:6).[20] As Carmen Imes writes:

> Why do they need a new covenant? The reason is clear. Not because there was something wrong with the Sinai covenant. Simply "because they broke my covenant." The problem was with the people...the covenant hasn't changed. It involves the

---

20   The author of Hebrews reaffirms Jeremiah's prophecy that the Torah would be written on the hearts of God's people in Hebrews 8:10. Some argue that the entirety of the Torah, including laws like the Sabbath, cannot possibly be what Jeremiah and the author of Hebrews have in mind, but instead, they must be thinking of a new law that doesn't include the Sabbath. But this idea is unreasonable. See Matthew Thiessen, "Hebrews and the Jewish Law," *So Great A Salvation: A Dialogue on the Atonement in Hebrews*, ed. Jon C. Laansma, George H. Guthrie, and Cynthia Westfall (London: T&T Clark, 2019), 184-185: "[I]f it is a priori unthinkable that Hebrews' use of Jer. 38:33 LXX [Jer. 31:33 MT] could include the entirety of the Jewish law, then it must be just as unthinkable that the prophet Jeremiah could have intended his prophecy to refer to the entirety of the Jewish law, rituals included. But we have no evidence that Jeremiah thought that such a New Covenant entailed the obsolescence of ritual and cultic laws or that other early Jews understood this passage to hint at such an obsolescence of the law. So how, apart from certain Christian presuppositions, can we conclude that Hebrews does? ... there simply is no evidence in Hebrews that the author rejects the ritual and cultic aspects of the Jewish law. Rather, there is strong evidence that he thinks these aspects of the law remain in effect at the time of his writing."

same partners and the same law. The difference is that God will enable every Israelite to internalize it. Yahweh said earlier that "Judah's sin is engraved with an iron tool…on the tablets of their hearts" (Jeremiah 17:1). Their sin occupies the center of their thinking, feeling, and decision making. When the covenant is renewed, their center of gravity will be the Torah instead: It will be written on their hearts.[21]

The fourth problem with the idea that the Sabbath doesn't apply to Gentile believers because it is part of an obsolete covenant is that the Sinai Covenant is not actually obsolete. The Sinai Covenant is one of the "covenants of promise" that Gentile believers in Messiah are no longer strangers to (Ephesians 2:12, 19).[22]

Now, it is certainly common to hear prominent Christian pastors like Andy Stanley proclaim, "The author of Hebrews says the new covenant rendered the old and everything associated with it *obsolete*."[23] For Stanley, Hebrews 8 teaches that the Messiah's coming abrogated the Sinai Covenant and the Torah. But even if Hebrews 8 *did* teach that the Sinai Covenant was made obsolete, that still would not mean that

---

21 Carmen Imes, *Bearing God's Name: Why Sinai Still Matters* (InterVarsity Press, 2019), 128-129.

22 See A.T. Lincoln, *Ephesians: Word Biblical Commentary 42* (Grand Rapids, MI: Zondervan, 1990), 137: "The writer probably has in mind a series of covenants—with Abraham (Gen 15:7–21, 17:1–21), with Isaac (Gen 26:2–5), with Jacob (Gen 28:13–15), with Israel (Exod 24:1–8), and with David (2 Sam 7). All can be seen as based on promise: the promises of God's presence, of descendants, and of the land, which were so essential to Israel's existence…Previously, then, the Gentiles were outside the line of promise, but, as the writer will point out in 3:6, they now participate in the promise through Christ (cf. also 1:13).

23 Andy Stanley, *Irresistible: Reclaiming the New that Jesus Unleashed for the World* (Grand Rapids, MI: Zondervan, 2018), 153.

the Torah was also made obsolete. As we saw above, the Torah and the Sabbath are not dependent upon the Sinai Covenant and are written on believers' hearts in the New Covenant. Nevertheless, a closer look at the book of Hebrews reveals that the Sinai Covenant was *not* rendered obsolete.

> But as it is, Christ has obtained a ministry that is as much more excellent than the old as the covenant he mediates is better, since it is enacted on better promises. For if that first covenant had been faultless, there would have been no occasion to look for a second.
> —Hebrews 8:6-7

Commenting on this passage, Andy Stanley writes, "This is an extraordinary and unsettling statement. Apparently there was something wrong with the old covenant."[24] But does this passage really say that there was something wrong with the Sinai Covenant? Not in the original Greek. As R.L. Watson points out, the phrase "the old" in Hebrews 8:6 "is not in the original Greek or any textual variants."[25] Watson goes on to explain that the word "covenant" in verses 7 and 13 of Hebrews 8 also does not appear in the original Greek but was added by translators. When we read these verses without the added words, it significantly impacts how the text can be read:

---

24 Stanley, *Irresistible*, 152.

25 R.L. Watson, *Forgotten Covenant* (Port Orchard, WA: Ark House Press, 2021), 239-240: "The original text for verse six can be best rendered as: 'But now He has obtained a more excellent ministry, by as much as He is also the mediator of a better covenant.' Thus, the translators have added 'old' to the translated text. So, to say that this passage is even talking about 'the old covenant' is inaccurate."

And when we read these verses, in context, without the added words, it becomes apparent the author of Hebrews wasn't even trying to compare the totality of the Mosaic Covenant with the New Covenant...after discussing the superiority of Christ's High Priestly ministry into the Heavenly Places over those who minister in the Temple in verses 1-5, the author has said that Christ has a greater ministry. This is the context. What this means is that when the author continues, he is saying that because of the faultiness of the first ministry, a second superior ministry (Christ's) was needed. The ministry of the priests who served in the Tabernacle and Temple was sufficient for its earthly and temporal purpose, however, it did nothing for humanity's sinful condition. Indeed, it was never intended to do so.[26]

It appears that the author of Hebrews is not comparing the Sinai Covenant with the New Covenant in Hebrews 8. He is comparing the earthly priesthood with Messiah's heavenly priesthood. The overall context, chapters 7-10, is all about this comparison. The fault is not with the covenant but with the Levitical ministry. In fact, the author's statement in Hebrews 8:7 is a reiteration of one of his earlier statements:

For if that first [ministry] had been faultless, there would have been no occasion to look for a second.
—Hebrews 8:7

---

26   Ibid., 240.

> Now if perfection had been attainable through the Levitical
> priesthood…what further need would there have been for
> another priest to arise…
> —Hebrews 7:11

This parallel further suggests that the author's point in this section is to compare ministries. Again, the fault is not with the Sinai Covenant; the fault is with the earthly Levitical priests. That is why in verse 8, right before the author quotes Jeremiah, he says, "For he finds fault with *them*…" (Hebrews 8:8, emphasis added). The author does not say he finds fault with *it*, that is, the covenant. No, he says he finds fault with *them*.

What is wrong with the Levitical priesthood? As the author explains, the Levitical Priesthood has a legitimate role serving in the earthly tabernacle (Hebrews 8:3-5). The issue, however, is that Levitical priests are human. They have weaknesses, they sin, and grow old and die (Hebrews 5:2; 7:22-23, 28; 9:7). Because of this, their sacrifices cannot truly deal with humanity's sinful condition (Hebrews 9:9-10; 10:11). Only the sinless and immortal heavenly High Priest can accomplish this (Hebrews 7:11). Only the Messiah can inaugurate the New Covenant, make complete atonement for sins, and enable the Torah to be written on the hearts of God's people in accordance with the New Covenant promises (Hebrews 8:10, 12; cf. Jeremiah 31:33-34). The author's point is that the Levitical Priesthood cannot do what only the Messiah's superior heavenly priesthood is designed to do.

Now that we see that the author is comparing the earthly and heavenly priesthoods, and not the Sinai and New covenants, we can understand what he means in verse 13:

> In speaking of a new [covenant], he makes the first one
> obsolete. And what is becoming obsolete and growing old is
> ready to vanish away.
> —Hebrews 8:13

Remember, the word "covenant" is not actually in the Greek text here. As Watson writes:

> Now, this insertion of 'covenant' is not completely dishonest
> since the context of quoting Jeremiah 31 means it was a
> reference to the New Covenant. But why was it left out here?
> It seems that by leaving it out, the author of Hebrews was
> reinforcing that what was in view here was a comparison of
> ministries, not covenants. Thus, here, as in verse 7, 'the first'
> that was faulty and becoming obsolete is the earthly priestly
> ministry, and not the Law, nor the Mosaic Covenant, with the
> destruction of the Temple in 70 AD.[27]

So, what does the author of Hebrews say is "becoming obsolete and growing old and ready to vanish away"? Once again, it is not the Sinai Covenant. *It is the earthly priesthood.*

Consider the historical context. We know from the gospel accounts that there was corruption within the priesthood. Some Jewish sects, like the Qumran community, protested the Jerusalem temple because they believed it had become irredeemably corrupt. So, we can assume that many people at this time recognized that the earthly priesthood was not functioning the way it was supposed to because of fallen men.

---

27   Ibid., 242.

During his earthly ministry, Yeshua even prophesied the temple's eventual destruction (Luke 21:5-6), which occurred in 70 AD.

The book of Hebrews was likely written in the early 80's AD, some years after the temple was destroyed.[28] For a short time after the temple's destruction, we know from Josephus (*Contra Apion.* 2.6.23) and the Mishnah (m.*Pesachim* 7.2) that the priesthood still functioned in a limited capacity, but they no longer offered public sacrifices. They were, as it says in Hebrews 8:13, "ready to vanish away." As Alexander Guttmann writes:

> When the Temple was destroyed in 70 CE, the public sacrifices were completely terminated. However, some of the private sacrifices were, for a short period, still offered on a limited scale. With the possible exception of Gamaliel II, no rabbi is known to have offered any sacrifice after 70 CE. However, the cessation of the sacrificial cult was not an inevitable consequence of the destruction of the Temple as shown in the light of past precedents.[29]

Considering the historical situation, it is easy to see why the author of Hebrews felt the need to explain what God's people should do without an earthly priesthood. It was literally about to cease to exist. What's more, the Greek phrase "he has made obsolete" (*pepalaioken*) in Hebrews 8:13 does not mean to abolish or cancel. Instead, it has the meaning of wearing out, no longer able to function as designed.[30] This

---

28 Simon J. Kistemaker, *Exposition of the Epistle of the Hebrews* (Grand Rapids, MI: Baker, 1984), 14-16.

29 Alexander Guttmann, "The End of the Sacrificial Jewish Cult" *HUCA* 38 (1967), 147.

30 H.G. Liddell and R. Scott, *A Greek-English Lexicon* (Oxford: Clarendon Press, 1996), 1290.

same word is used earlier in Hebrews to describe garments that have become worn out (Hebrews 1:11). Within the historical circumstances in which the author of Hebrews wrote, the earthly priesthood could not function the way it was designed to function.

The author of Hebrews is writing to encourage his readers to stay faithful to the Messiah (Hebrews 10:32-34). He is trying to reassure them that, even if the temple is destroyed and the priesthood can't function the way it was intended, it is okay. We have a great High Priest serving in the heavenly tabernacle. The earthly priesthood is a shadow of the heavenly reality. So regardless of what happens with the earthly temple and priesthood, the Messiah's heavenly High Priesthood endures forever. Again, he does not teach that the Sinai Covenant or Torah is faulty or abolished, but rather affirms Jeremiah's prophecy about the Torah being written on the heart (Hebrews 8:10). What is growing old and ready to vanish away in Hebrews 8:13 is not the Sinai Covenant but rather the earthly priesthood—it couldn't function as designed due to the historical circumstances.

In summary, the argument that the Sabbath doesn't apply to Gentile believers in the New Covenant fails for numerous reasons. First, God gave the Sabbath to all humanity at creation, long before the covenant was made with Israel at Mount Sinai. Second, Gentiles in Messiah are part of the commonwealth of Israel, so the Sabbath applies to them just as much as it applies to Jewish believers. Third, the New Covenant promise affirms the ongoing validity of the Sabbath commandment, including for Gentile believers. Fourth, while the Sabbath does not depend on the Sinai Covenant, the Sinai Covenant nevertheless was not rendered obsolete.

Conclusion

In this chapter, we learned that the idea that the Sabbath is only for Jews and not Gentiles is without biblical basis. Several Old and New Testament passages testify that the Sabbath commandment applies to both Jewish and Gentile believers. While many cite Acts 15 as evidence that the apostles exempted Gentile believers from laws like the Sabbath, we saw that, in reality, this passage addresses the separate issue of ritual conversion for salvation. The apostles taught that Gentile believers did not need to convert to Judaism to be saved and received into the community, but it was assumed that the Gentile believers would continue to learn the Torah every Sabbath as they attended synagogue services. We also saw that the Sabbath is applicable in the New Covenant; it was given to mankind at the beginning, believing Gentiles are part of the commonwealth of Israel, and the New Covenant writes the Torah (including the Sabbath) on the hearts of believers, including Gentile believers.

CHAPTER 5
SABBATH FAQS

This chapter focuses on answering Sabbath-related questions that weren't directly relevant to what was addressed in previous chapters. I will cover not only theological but also practical questions about Sabbath observance. I pray that the earlier chapters of this book have persuaded you that the Sabbath is still important for Christians. While I can't cover everything,[1] hopefully this chapter will help address many of your questions.

How do we observe the Sabbath biblically?

While Pharisaic and later rabbinic Judaism has come up with many Sabbath prohibitions (e.g., m.*Shabbat*), the Bible itself gives only a few. For instance, Exodus 20:10 commands us not to "do any work." The Hebrew word translated "work" (*m'lachah*) basically refers to "one's routine or habitual work, i.e., one's business."[2] That is, whatever one does for self-provision. For most people today, this "work" would mean their regular job by which they make an income. So, on the seventh day (Friday evening to Saturday evening), we don't do whatever it is we usually do for self-provision (i.e., our regular job). We take the day off.

Additionally, the command not to "work" would include things like yardwork and household chores. Exodus 20:8 says, "Six days you shall labor, and do all your work." Labor (*abad, aboda*) is directly tied to things like agricultural work in fields and vineyards (Deuteronomy

---

1   For further study, see J. K. McKee, *Messianic Sabbath Helper*, Margaret Huey, ed. (McKinney, TX: Messianic Apologetics, 2015).

2   R. Laird Harris, Gleason L. Archer, Bruce K. Waltke, *Theological Wordbook of the Old Testament* (Chicago: Moody Press, 1980), 465.

28:39; 2 Samuel 9:10; Proverbs 12:11; 28:19) and repairing the temple (2 Chronicles 34:13). While many people today might not have actual fields, the principle is that the Sabbath should be a day of complete rest, a day to cease from ordinary household responsibilities. Mowing the lawn, cleaning the house, etc., can be done on the other six days of the week.

Other Sabbath prohibitions include not lighting a fire for work purposes on the Sabbath[3] (Exodus 35:3). Jeremiah 17:19-23 indicates that we are not to buy or sell on the Sabbath (cf. Nehemiah 13:15-17). This prohibition might be elaborating on the Torah's command to allow your servants to rest on the Sabbath (Exodus 20:10). In other words, we must not directly cause anyone else to work for us on the Sabbath day. As one example, we should avoid going out to eat at restaurants and having cooks and servers prepare and serve us food. Finally, Isaiah 58:13 prohibits doing one's "own pleasure" on the Sabbath. This phrase is much fraught over, but it is exegetically straightforward. Isaiah 58:3-4 explains what "seeking your own pleasure" is: "Before, in the day of your fast you *seek your own pleasure*, and oppress all your workers. Behold, you fast only to quarrel and to fight and to hit with a wicked fist (emphasis added)." Seeking your own pleasure means doing what you want, i.e., sinning (including mistreating other people), rather than doing what God wants, i.e., obeying his commandments and loving other people. Instead of pursuing our own sinful agenda on the Sabbath, we should seek God's purposes for the day (rest, worship, family time, community, etc.). The command not to do our own pleasure cannot mean that we aren't allowed to do

---

3   I elaborate on this prohibition in this chapter under the heading "Are we prohibited from lighting a fire on the Sabbath?"

pleasurable things on the Sabbath because the same verse says that we must take delight in the Sabbath.[4]

What about what we *should* do on the Sabbath? First, Exodus 20:8 commands us to *remember* the Sabbath day. That means don't forget about it! We must make the Sabbath part of our lives and plan our schedules accordingly.

Second, Exodus 20:8 also tells us to sanctify the Sabbath, to "keep it holy." Generally, the Sabbath is to be treated as different from the other six days of the week. It is a special day dedicated to the Lord. What makes the Sabbath special is that it is a day of rest (Exodus 20:8-9); thus, we keep the Sabbath holy by treating it as a day of rest. There are some additional ways we can make the Sabbath special on a personal level. Many people implement traditional prayers and rituals into their Sabbath observance.[5] These traditions are not required in Scripture, but many people have found them to be helpful in making the Sabbath a special day for their families.

Third, Exodus 23:12 says that we are to "rest" on the seventh day. The Hebrew word for "rest" here is *shabat* (the root of the word *Sabbath*), which means "to cease."[6] Just as God ceased from his work on the Sabbath (Genesis 2:3), humans are to put aside our work and con-

---

4 See Ed Christian, "Sabbath Is a Happy Day! What Does Isaiah 58:13-14 Mean?" *JATS* 13/1 (Spring 2002): 81-90: "The Hebrew word translated 'delight,' found twice in verses 13-14, is oneg, which means 'exquisite delight,' 'dainty,' 'soft,' and 'delicate.' It sometimes refers to luxury, what is rich and delicious, like Sabbath dinner. That's God's intention for the Sabbath! It should be the most exquisite, luxuriously delightful day of the week! Isn't that better than 'your own pleasure'? But if the Sabbath is an 'exquisite delight' for us, are we not taking pleasure in it?"

5 For a simple overview of these traditions, see David Wilber, *A Christian Guide to the Biblical Feasts* (Saint Charles, MO: Freedom Hill Community, 2018).

6 R. Laird Harris, Gleason L. Archer, Bruce K. Waltke, *Theological Wordbook of the Old Testament* (Chicago: Moody Press, 1980), 902.

cerns of regular life. The Sabbath is an invitation to stop, to recalibrate, and reprioritize our lives around what matters most—our God and our families and the people we love. We weren't created to work our lives away, to immerse ourselves in nothing but life's daily drudgery. God gave us the gift of rest. Another word translated "rest," found in Exodus 20:11, is the verb *nuach*, which means to "rest, settle down and remain."[7] The Sabbath is a time to stop whatever work we are doing, regardless of how important we think it might be at the time, and to enjoy God's gift of rest.

Fourth, Leviticus 23:3 calls the Sabbath a holy gathering. The implication is that believers should gather together on the Sabbath for worship and fellowship. This was the custom of Yeshua and the apostles (e.g., Luke 4:16; Acts 17:1-2). The author of Hebrews says, "Let us consider how to stir up one another to love and good works, not neglecting to meet together, as is the habit of some, but encouraging one another, and all the more as you see the Day drawing near" (Hebrews 10:24-25). God intended the Sabbath to be a joyful time for believers to meet together and encourage one another. We must not neglect this holy gathering.

Fifth, we are to reflect on how God is the creator of all things. Exodus 20:11 teaches that the Sabbath is a memorial of creation. This magnificent universe didn't just pop into existence from nothing. No, an intelligent designer of the cosmos is behind it all. We affirm our commitment to this truth every time we rest on the seventh day. Observing the Sabbath is a way of acknowledging that God is sovereign over all creation. He created the universe for his purposes. Our lives

---

7   Francis Brown, S. Driver, and C. Briggs, *Hebrew and English Lexicon of the Old Testament* (Oxford: Clarendon Press, 1979), 628.

and our time are not our own. We submit to his sovereignty by resting when he says to rest.

Sixth, we are to reflect on how God is our redeemer. The Sabbath is a memorial not only of creation but also of Israel's deliverance from slavery in Egypt (Deuteronomy 5:15). This truth is revealed more fully in the Messiah, who delivered us from slavery to sin and death. When we observe the Sabbath, we recognize that redemption and freedom are found only in the Lord.

Seventh, we have the privilege of taking delight in the Sabbath. It is a day God gave to mankind as a gift for our benefit (Mark 2:27). It is a day intended to "refresh" those who observe it (Exodus 31:17). God did not intend the Sabbath to be a burden but rather a time of joy. The Bible says that blessings come when we honor the Sabbath and call it a delight (Isaiah 58:13). There is some freedom in how we can fulfill this broad principle of delighting in the Sabbath.[8] Ask the Holy Spirit for guidance.

How do we know that the Sabbath is from sundown Friday to sundown Saturday?

Biblical days begin and end at sundown. We see this at the beginning of creation. Genesis 1:5 says, "And there was evening and there was morning, the first day." The first "day" included the dark part and light part, and the dark part of the day came first. The same is true for the other days of the week (Genesis 1:8, 13, 19, 23, 31). Additionally,

---

8   People often ask if a husband and wife are allowed to make love on the Sabbath. The answer is yes. Doubts about intimacy being permissible on the Sabbath usually arise from a misunderstanding of Isaiah's command not to do one's own pleasure (see footnote #4 in this chapter). Historically, only a few small sectarian Jewish communities in the Second Temple era discouraged sex on the Sabbath (e.g., Jubilees 50:7). Rabbinic Judaism encourages making love on the Sabbath (m.*Ketubot* 5.1; b.*Ketubot* 62b).

Leviticus 23:27 says that Yom Kippur is the tenth "day" of the seventh month. Yet, Leviticus 23:32 says that Yom Kippur begins at sundown on the ninth of the month. This indicates that the ninth day of the month is ending at sundown as the tenth day of the month is beginning: "from evening to evening shall you keep your Sabbath." Nehemiah 13:19 also indicates that the weekly Sabbath begins at sundown. Nehemiah orders the people to shut the gates "as it began to grow dark" to prevent the merchants from buying and selling on the Sabbath. If the day began and ended at sunrise, the merchants would still have had plenty of time to buy and sell before the Sabbath.

In addition to the biblical record, Josephus records that the Sabbath day lasted from sundown to sundown. He says that priests would sound the trumpet "at the beginning of every seventh day, in the evening twilight, as also at the evening when that day was finished" in order to notify the people "when they were to leave off work, and when they were to go to work again" (*Jewish Wars*, 4.9.12). The Mishnah also clearly indicates that the Sabbath is from sundown Friday to sundown Saturday. One passage prohibits Jews from giving "skins to a gentile tanner, nor clothes to a gentile launderer, unless there is sufficient time for work on them to be completed while it is still day, before Shabbat begins." Work is allowed to be done "as long as the sun is shining on Friday" (m.*Shabbat* 1.8).

Yeshua certainly knew when the Sabbath was, and according to the gospels, he observed the Sabbath on the same day as the rest of the Jewish people (e.g., Luke 4:16). From the first century to today, the Jewish people have been widely dispersed throughout the world. Jewish communities worldwide still observe the Sabbath from sundown Friday to sundown Saturday. There is no evidence that the Jewish people changed the timing of when they kept the Sabbath anytime between the first century to today.[9] Moreover, there is no historical record of any disputes between Jewish teachers or communities regarding when to observe the Sabbath, which certainly would have occurred had such a change been introduced.[10]

Are we prohibited from lighting a fire on the Sabbath?

Exodus 35:3 says, "You shall kindle no fire in all your dwelling places on the Sabbath day." That seems pretty cut and dried. Rabbinic Judaism has historically understood this command to be prohibiting "only the creation of a fire and such use of it as cooking and baking... but there is no prohibition against enjoying its light and heat."[11] In other words, a fire lit before the Sabbath could be left burning throughout the Sabbath day (as long as it isn't used for food preparation), but one cannot *actually light* the fire anytime during the Sabbath. Many

---

9   Roman historical sources from AD 70-229 consistently identify the Jewish day of rest (Sabbath) with their "day of Saturn," Saturday. See Frontinus, *Stratagem* 2.1.17; Cassius Dio, *Roman History* 37.16.1-4; 49.22.4-6; 65.7.2.

10   Some people on the religious fringes have proposed something called the "lunar Sabbath theory," which is the idea that the Sabbath is counted seven days from the new moon every month. This would mean that, in one month, the Sabbath might be on Thursday, but the next month it would be on a Sunday, and so forth. This theory should be rejected on the basis of historical evidence indicating that the Jewish people kept the Sabbath from Friday sundown to Saturday sundown from the first century (when Messiah kept it) to today. McKee also explains how the lunar Sabbath theory lacks any coherent logic: "What if there is a New Moon sighted on the sixth day of one's counting cycle to the Sabbath, and the counting cycle to the Sabbath has to be reinitiated? This would mean that it is possible for there not to be a Sabbath day of rest for a period of thirteen days" (J.K. McKee, *Messianic Sabbath Helper*, 171). For more on why the lunar Sabbath theory is lunacy, see 119 Ministries, "Time: The Lunar Sabbath Uncovered," *Test Everything*, www.testeverything.net.

11   Nosson Scherman, ed., *ArtScroll Chumash*, Stone Edition (Brooklyn: Mesorah Publications, Ltd., 2000), 517.

modern Orthodox Jews take this idea so far as to prohibit flipping on a light switch or starting a car.

It is possible that this prohibition against lighting a fire on the Sabbath is not a general restriction but was actually meant to apply specifically to the construction of the tabernacle.[12] According to Peter Enns, "In my opinion, 'lighting a fire' is too specific and unexpected a detail to refer simply to one particular type of work that might be done on the Sabbath."[13] Perhaps it is not a coincidence that this command occurs in the midst of the instructions concerning the tabernacle's construction—a massive project requiring much work, including work involving fire (Exodus 36:26; 37:3; 38:5, 27). As J.K. McKee writes, "[S]ome might conclude that a more restricted form of kindling a fire—for the purposes of metalworking or smelting, for example—might be more what v. 3 intends."[14] If this view is correct, then the prohibition against kindling a fire was a reminder to Israel to cease from working on the Sabbath, specifically in regard to the work required in constructing the tabernacle. However, one problem with this interpretation is that the verse says, "in all your dwelling places." According to McKee, "This would lend support to fire being used for household chores and food preparation."[15]

In any case, the commandment seems to prohibit kindling a fire for the purpose of doing some kind of work. The historical rabbinic view might be right that food preparation is in view. As R. Alan Cole notes, "Exodus 16:23 seems to imply that the sabbath supply of manna

12 See J.P. Hyatt, *Exodus* (New Century Bible, 1971), 329: "It may have been intended here to prohibit making a fire for the metalworking involved in constructing the Tabernacle and its furniture."

13 Peter Enns, *Exodus* (Grand Rapids, MI: Zondervan 2000), 545.

14 McKee, *Messianic Sabbath Helper*, 206.

15 Ibid.

must be cooked the night before."[16] Cooking food in ancient times took time and effort. People didn't have the luxury of being able to utilize modern conveniences like microwaves, where heating up leftovers is as simple as pressing a button. Douglas Stuart provides an excellent summary of the possible intention behind this instruction:

> The command "do not light a fire in any of your dwellings on the Sabbath day" is also a summational statement, a way of stating briefly that no work can be done on the Sabbath, as is clearly spelled out not only in the prior verse but in the prior passages on the Sabbath in chaps. 20 and 31. But what does lighting a fire have to do with working? The answer is that the simplest sort of work that anyone might be tempted to do on the Sabbath (within the category of prohibited work, work that must not be done, in fact) was cooking meals ... the Sabbath law recognized that either allowing or requiring the cooking of meals on the Sabbath would undeniably represent work for the women and/or servants of the family and thus represent a clear violation of the law.[17]

If this interpretation is correct, what might it mean for us in modern times? Once again, the prohibition against kindling a fire on the Sabbath seems to relate to doing work. Generally speaking, we should avoid engaging in work that involves using fire on the Sabbath. But applying this principle in our modern world will look differently than it did in ancient times. Using a microwave to heat food, starting a car engine (which involves sparks) to drive to Sabbath services, flipping

---

16   R. Alan Cole, *Exodus* (Downers Grove, IL: InterVarsity Press, 2016), 244.

17   Douglas K. Stuart, *Exodus* (Nashville: B&H Publishing Group, 2006), 749.

on a light switch, etc., do not really require work. Thus, doing these things does not seem to violate the principle of the commandment. I think J.K. McKee has the right approach:

> My personal opinion regarding this commandment is that in ancient times, it was major work to get a fire started ... But today we do live in a modern age when the technological level has changed our ability to manipulate "fire." The ancients did not have the ability to strike a match and ignite a gas fireplace with the ease that we have today. The ancients did not have electricity or microwave ovens ... Any proper Messianic interpretation of this commandment will take into consideration the progress of technology. I will say that I do not consider it a sin to drive on the Sabbath, or even microwave leftovers from the Shabbat meal the night before. But if I am engaging in strenuous work on the Sabbath, which involves fire, electricity, or my car, that is probably something else. We each have the responsibility to go to the Lord and see how this commandment is to be applied in our modern world.[18]

Some parts of the Torah have passed away, such as animal sacrifices and the Levitical priesthood. So, is it true to say that Matthew 5:18 affirms Sabbath observance?

Matthew 5:18 says, "For truly, I say to you, until heaven and earth pass away, not an iota, not a dot, will pass from the Law until all is accomplished." In chapter 1, I argued that this verse stresses the Torah's immutability. Not even the smallest detail of the Torah will pass away until heaven and earth pass away and all is accomplished, which is a

---

18   McKee, *Messianic Sabbath Helper*, 83.

reference to the end of time, when the present created universe passes away (2 Peter 3:7, 13; Revelation 21:1). If not even "the smallest stroke of the smallest letter" of the Torah has passed away, then neither has the Sabbath. Therefore, according to Matthew 5:18, the command to observe the Sabbath remains valid instruction for God's people.

However, could this verse actually mean something different than what it plainly says? Aren't there some parts of the Torah, like the laws governing the Levitical Priesthood and sacrifices, that *have* passed away in light of the Messiah's atoning work on the cross? Andrew Schumacher argues that since such laws have *obviously* become irrelevant, then the statement "until all has been accomplished" must have occurred when Yeshua died for our sins and is therefore different from the future time when "heaven and earth pass away." Thus, according to Schumacher, it is possible that laws like the Sabbath have already passed away:

> If any of the sacrifices are no longer necessary due to the sacrifice of Christ, even if it's just one small kind of sacrifice, then at least one letter has become non-binding, and thus has passed from the Law. If that is the case, then we are forced to take the phrase "until all is accomplished" to be fulfilled, and therefore most likely not speaking of the same time as "until heaven and earth pass away."[19]

Even if we grant Schumacher's assumption that some parts of the Torah have already passed away, it still wouldn't follow that the Sabbath has been done away with for Christians. After all, the Sabbath was established at creation, long before the Torah was given to Israel

---

19   Andrew Schumacher, "Matthew 5 and the Hebrew Roots Movement, verse 18," *Beginning of Wisdom*. www.beginningwisdom.org.

at Mount Sinai (Genesis 2:2-3). Yeshua affirmed the Sabbath's validity when he declared that it was made for mankind's benefit (Mark 2:27). Isaiah prophesied that all mankind will observe the Sabbath in the new heavens and new earth (Isaiah 66:23). Even if some commandments from the Torah have already passed away, there is still no reason to think that the Sabbath was one of them.

However, Schumacher's assumption has some flaws. First, the two clauses in the verse ("until heaven and earth pass away" and "until all is accomplished") undoubtedly refer to the same event. The obvious problem with interpreting the second clause, "until all is accomplished," as referring to a separate earlier event (such as when Yeshua accomplished his work on the cross) is that it "plainly contradicts the meaning of the first clause, which refers to the ongoing validity of the law until the end of the age."[20] Donald Hagner has the correct approach, which is to "take the clauses as essentially synonymous."[21] The simple explanation for why the gospel writer included the additional clause is that "the repetition emphasizes a most important point for the evangelist: the law remains in place until the consummation of the age."[22]

Second, the apostles didn't think that the sacrifices and Levitical priesthood were nullified. Several passages indicate that they continued to participate in the Levitical services long after Yeshua's death and resurrection (Acts 2:46; 3:1; 21:26). The author of Hebrews himself recognizes the ongoing validity of the Levitical priesthood (Hebrews 8:4-5). Furthermore, both Ezekiel and Zechariah acknowledge the reality of a future earthly priesthood, temple, Levites, and sacrifices during the millennial reign of Messiah (Ezekiel 40-48; Zechariah 14:20-21).

---

20 Donald A. Hagner, *Matthew 1-13* (Word Biblical Commentary, 1993), 107.
21 Ibid.
22 Ibid.

To be clear, Yeshua is the High Priest of a greater priesthood in heaven, as Hebrews clearly teaches. He is the ultimate sacrifice for our sins. The Levitical priesthood could not attain perfection because it was made up of fallen men, and animal sacrifices could not truly provide atonement because they could not provide the payment for sin that only the Messiah's sacrifice could fulfill (Hebrews 7:11, 22-23, 28; 10:4). But it doesn't follow from any of these facts that the Levitical priesthood has been nullified. The Levitical priesthood has *always* functioned as the earthly shadow that points to the heavenly reality. It will function in that role again during the millennial reign. Until then, because no early temple or priesthood exists, there is no way to observe the parts of the Torah governing the priesthood. So, in the meantime, we do our best to keep the parts of the Torah that we are able to keep while anticipating the day when Messiah returns. At that time, we will be able to observe the Torah more fully.

Our modern situation in this regard is similar to the time Israel was in exile in Babylon. The fact that they couldn't keep the commandments pertaining to the sacrificial system didn't nullify those commandments. Once they returned to the land and rebuilt the temple, they started keeping them again. Thus, the fact that some parts of the Torah are impossible to keep in our current situation does not mean that those parts of the Torah have passed away. And it certainly does not mean that the Sabbath has passed away.[23]

---

23 For more on understanding the Levitical priesthood and sacrifices from a pronomian (pro-law) perspective, see Tim Hegg, *Why We Keep Torah: 10 Persistent Questions* (Tacoma, WA: TorahResource, 2009), 25-36.

How should we understand Yeshua's comments about fleeing on the Sabbath in Matthew 24:20?

While often overlooked, Matthew 24:20 gives additional evidence of the Sabbath's enduring relevance to Christians. During his teaching concerning the coming destruction of Jerusalem in Matthew 24, Yeshua admonished his followers who would be caught in the middle of the war at that time to pray. Curiously, what he told them to pray involves the Sabbath: "Pray that your flight may not be in winter or on a Sabbath" (Matthew 24:20).

Again, Yeshua had in view the coming war and destruction of Jerusalem (Matthew 24:2-3), which occurred decades after he gave this instruction. Yeshua's followers in Jerusalem and Judea were to pray that they wouldn't have to flee in winter or on the Sabbath during this time. Why?

The reference to winter is easy to understand. Travel during the winter season was problematic for several reasons.[24] Given the additional difficulties that fleeing in the winter would provide, it makes sense that Yeshua would not want his followers to have to flee during that time of year. But why did Yeshua tell his followers to pray that they wouldn't have to flee on the Sabbath? In what way would fleeing on the Sabbath be considered less-than-ideal?

---

24   Craig Keener, *NIV Cultural Backgrounds Study Bible: Bringing to Life the Ancient World of Scripture* (Grand Rapids, MI: Zondervan, 2016): "In Judea, winter was the rainy season, and otherwise dry creek beds could flood with water from the mountains; cold winter rains also buried some roads in mud. The Jordan River also flooded, making it harder to cross; Josephus reports that even in the spring of AD 68 Judean fugitives were trapped by the flooding Jordan and thus slaughtered by their pursuers (Josephus, Wars 4.433). Armies normally withdrew from battle during the winter; travel was particularly dangerous in the cold mountains."

Numerous scholars suggest that many of Yeshua's followers during the time of Jerusalem's destruction in 70 AD still observed the Sabbath. Therefore, Yeshua's hope was that their observance of the Sabbath wouldn't be interrupted during the coming times of war. According to Donald Hagner, "While the point of the reference to the Sabbath is hardly clear, probably what is meant is that an urgent flight on the Sabbath would make any Sabbath observance impossible."[25] William Shea remarks similarly:

> Christians were exhorted to pray that their flight, at the
> beginning of the Roman war, would not have to occur on the
> Sabbath out of respect for their observance of that day. They
> could flee on that day if they had to, but they were to pray that
> they would not in order to keep that day as one of rest and
> worship, rather than a day of travel.[26]

Tim Hegg agrees with this interpretation and gives insight into why an attack on the Sabbath would present additional challenges:

> [T]he reason one would hope that an attack would not take
> place on Shabbat would be the interruption of the sacred
> day itself as well the difficulty that members of the family
> might not be in close proximity to each other. For example,
> mothers with infants to care for might have remained at home
> while their husbands attended the Shabbat meeting in the
> synagogue. Given such a scenario, one could well imagine
> that an attack on Shabbat would cause even greater disruption

---

25   Donald A. Hagner, *Matthew 14-28* (Dallas: Word Biblical Commentary, 1995), 701-702.
26   William Shea, "The Sabbath in Matthew 24:20," *AUSS* Vol. 40, No. 1 (2002), 35.

among families as they were separated from each other in their attempts to flee the city.[27]

Again, these proposed reasons that flight on the Sabbath would be less-than-ideal are based on the assumption that Yeshua's followers would be keeping the Sabbath. Given these considerations, what Yeshua's instructions imply is that he expected continued Sabbath observance among his followers in the future. He did not intend his followers to derive the idea from any of his teachings that the Sabbath was no longer important. As Shea writes:

> [I]t appears that Jesus was giving his believers advice that they were to pray that they would still be able to keep the Sabbath even in those coming times of war. This in turn suggests that Jesus considered the Sabbath to be binding upon Christians of that future time.[28]

Craig Evans cites this verse as another example of Yeshua upholding the Law of God, which of course includes the command to keep the Sabbath: "By having Jesus urge his disciples to pray that the day of emergency not occur 'on a Sabbath,' Jesus is once again seen as upholding the Law (cf. Matt 5:17-20)."[29] Skip MacCarty also comments on the implications of Yeshua's instructions in Matthew 24:20: "Jesus' instruction safeguarding the quality of His followers' Sabbath observance would be expected of one who assumed the universal and

---

27   Tim Hegg, *Matthew Chapters 24-28* (Tacoma, WA: TorahResource, 2013), 1111.

28   William Shea, "The Sabbath in Matthew 24:20," 23.

29   Craig A. Evans, *Matthew* (Cambridge University Press, 2012), 406.

permanent character of the Sabbath."[30] For good measure, Walter Specht also puts it well:

> [I]f this is a genuine dominical saying, it indicates that our Lord expected His followers to regard the Sabbath as sacred as late as the destruction of Jerusalem in A.D. 70. He instructed them to pray that at that time of crisis they would not find it necessary to flee on the Sabbath. But the implication is that conditions could be such as to make instant flight necessary even on the day of rest. But the fear, bustle, and confusion that a hasty flight on Sabbath would bring were not in harmony with the worship, peace, and joy that should characterize the sacred day of rest. Hence, Jesus' followers were urged to pray that the flight would occur on a different day of the week.[31]

There are two other common interpretations of this passage. In contrast to the perspective outlined above, these alternative interpretations do not require us to believe that Yeshua's followers within Matthew's community were still faithful to the Sabbath. However, as we will see, these alternative interpretations fail to provide an adequate explanation of Yeshua's mention of the Sabbath.

The first alternative interpretation is that fleeing the city on the Sabbath would be difficult due to certain physical challenges Yeshua's followers would encounter. For instance, it is believed that the gates of Jerusalem would have been shut on the Sabbath (Nehemiah 13:19-

---

30   Skip MacCarty, "The Seventh-Day Sabbath," *Perspectives on the Sabbath: 4 Views*, Christopher Donato, ed. (Nashville, TN: B& H Academic, 2011), 23.

31   Walter F. Specht, "The Sabbath in the New Testament," *The Sabbath in Scripture and History*, Kenneth A. Strand, ed. (Washington, DC: Review and Herald, 1982), 103.

20), making it difficult to leave the city. Also, stores would be closed, making it hard to purchase supplies for travel. Therefore, Yeshua's concern wasn't so much with his followers being able to observe the Sabbath. Instead, his concern had more to do with the external obstacles that would be in their way at that time. However, when looked at in detail, these supposed physical obstacles to flight would not have been significant considerations. For instance, as William Shea explains, the gates of Jerusalem were usually open on the Sabbath, and in times of war, the gates were closed every day:

> In peacetime [the gates] had to be open on Sabbath to enable worshipers to enter the temple precincts. In at least two instances the eastern gates of the temple also served as the eastern gates to the city. This was the case for the Golden Gate, blocked up from the time of Suleiman the Magnificent in the sixteenth century, and for the Sheep Gate through which the sacrifices for the temple were brought. Those coming from the eastern side of the city to worship in the temple precincts on Sabbath would have entered the city through these gates that were kept open in peacetime ... In times of war, all of the gates were closed all of the time, including the Sabbath.[32]

Given these facts, it is unlikely that Yeshua's mention of the Sabbath was because he was concerned about the city gates being closed, since they would have been closed every day during times of war. Additionally, people would still be able to flee despite the gates being closed.[33] The fact that the gates would have been closed every day

---

32 William Shea, "The Sabbath in Matthew 24:20," 31.
33 Ibid, 32: "The physical obstacles to a mandatory flight on the Sabbath day would have

during wartime, not just on the Sabbath, indicates that the gates were not Yeshua's primary concern when highlighting the Sabbath in his instructions to pray.

Regarding the idea that Yeshua would be concerned about his followers not being able to purchase supplies on the Sabbath, this concern would have applied to *any* day, not just the Sabbath. Yeshua explicitly says that there wouldn't even be enough time to take what is in one's house or turn back to grab one's cloak when it was time to flee (Matthew 24:17-18). Yeshua's followers were to escape with whatever they had on them. Furthermore, one wouldn't need supplies to flee for one day, and provisions could be purchased the following day if needed. Once again, this suggestion doesn't adequately explain Yeshua's mention of the Sabbath in Matthew 24:20.

The second common interpretation of this passage is that Yeshua was concerned that his followers fleeing on the Sabbath would invite persecution from the Jews. In other words, Yeshua wasn't concerned so much with his followers being able to observe the Sabbath; he was concerned about his followers being persecuted by their Jewish opponents over perceived violations of the Sabbath when they fled.

However, this second option is also unlikely. First, it presupposes that Yeshua's followers were no longer keeping the Sabbath. However, every indication from the New Testament is that Yeshua's followers remained faithful to the Sabbath even after his death and resurrection. The Book of Acts records several instances of the apostles and other followers of Yeshua observing the Sabbath alongside the broader Jewish

---

been minimal. People from inside of Jerusalem could have exited through the eastern gates of the temple, which also served as gates of the city. Other gates probably were open in peacetime to permit worshipers to take the most direct route to the temple area. Having cleared the Mount of Olives, travelers would have encountered no obstructions in their path down to Jericho other than the problem of having to traverse a barren area."

community (Acts 13:13-52; 17:2; 18:4). Second, this interpretation presupposes that fleeing on the Sabbath would have been offensive to the broader Jewish community. However, when we consider the historical Jewish sources, we discover that the generally held view among the Jewish people was that the Torah allowed for a suspending of the Sabbath to preserve life.[34]

Since Jewish people of the day believed that the Torah permitted someone to save his own life on the Sabbath, it seems reasonable that the Jews themselves "would have joined in that flight had they seen the threat in the same way."[35] Given these facts, Yeshua's followers fleeing on the Sabbath would not have antagonized their Jewish opponents, who would likely have joined them in their flight.

Now, as I pointed out earlier, numerous Christian scholars agree that Matthew's original readers continued to keep the Sabbath and that Matthew 24:20 may imply the Sabbath has continuing relevance. However, some might say that since Matthew's original audience was primarily made up of Jewish Christians that Yeshua's instructions in Matthew 24:20 are not intended for anyone beyond his Jewish followers. This objection can be countered in two ways.

First, if we can dismiss *some* of Yeshua's teaching because the original audience of Matthew's gospel was Jewish, then what is to stop us from dismissing *any* or *all* of his teaching in Matthew's gospel? The Sermon on the Mount was originally given to a Jewish audience and recorded in a gospel with an original Jewish readership. Should we throw that out? Of course not. There is no good reason to dismiss the implications of Matthew 24:20 just because Matthew's original audience was Jewish.

---

34   1 Maccabees 2:39-41; Josephus, *Antiquities* 14.63; b.*Shabbat* 19a.

35   William Shea, "The Sabbath in Matthew 24:20," 30.

Second, while originally written for a Jewish audience, Matthew's gospel itself indicates that the teaching contained therein is meant for all who follow Yeshua. Matthew records Yeshua's command to make disciples of "all nations" and to teach them to observe all that Yeshua commanded (Matthew 28:19-20). This fact shows that Matthew intended the teaching contained in his gospel to reach beyond the Jewish people.

In summary, it appears most likely that Yeshua's primary concern in admonishing his followers to pray that they would not need to flee on the Sabbath is the disruption of the Sabbath itself that such a flight would cause. Yeshua did not come to do away with the Sabbath but reaffirmed its validity and sacredness. Fleeing on the Sabbath would interfere with the Sabbath's peace and joy; therefore, Yeshua's followers should pray that any flight on the Sabbath could be avoided—even though they could flee on that day if they had to. These instructions addressed to his followers of that future time implies that Yeshua presupposed the Sabbath's ongoing relevance for his followers decades after his death and resurrection.

If the Sabbath is so important, why isn't it commanded in the New Testament?

It is often said that the commandment to observe the Sabbath is not repeated in the New Testament. Therefore, the Sabbath is not relevant to Christians. As MacArthur argues:

> There is never a command in the New Testament to keep
> the Sabbath. All Ten Commandments are repeated in the
> New Testament—some numerous times—except the fourth
> command. It is never repeated in the New Testament, not one
> single time. It was, in the midst of the moral law, a sign and

a symbol to lead the people to rest and repentance. But when you come to the New Testament, there's never a repeat of that command. The rest that the New Testament is concerned about is the rest that comes to the soul from hearing and believing the good news preached. That's the rest the New Testament offers.[36]

There are a couple of problems with this argument. First, even if we grant MacArthur's assumption that the New Testament does not reinforce Sabbath observance for Christians, that still would not mean that the Sabbath is irrelevant. For instance, the New Testament never explicitly reiterates the Torah's commandments against necromancy or bestiality, but obviously that does not mean that those commandments are done away with. We know that we shouldn't practice necromancy or bestiality because of the Old Testament. Similarly, the Old Testament is clear that followers of the God of Israel are to observe the Sabbath. Why should we think that *only* the New Testament is profitable for training in righteousness (2 Timothy 3:16)?

Second, MacArthur's assumption is wrong. As we saw in chapter 1, the New Testament reinforces the commandment to keep the Sabbath in numerous ways. Yeshua affirmed the Sabbath's ongoing validity in Matthew 5:19 when he admonished his followers to do and teach even the least of the Torah's commandments. All of the New Testament's exhortations to keep the Torah/commandments certainly include the Sabbath.[37] Moreover, the word for "Sabbath rest" in Hebrews 4:9 is *sabbatismos*, which is a technical term that refers to the literal act of

---

36   John MacArthur, "Understanding the Sabbath," *Grace to You*. www.gty.org.

37   Matthew 19:17; John 14:15, 21; 15:10; 1 Corinthians 7:19; 1 John 2:3-4; 3:22-24; 5:2-3; Revelation 14:12.

resting on the Sabbath day.[38] According to Hebrews 4:9, this Sabbath rest (observance) "remains" for the people of God, which indicates that the author of Hebrews expects his readers to literally observe the Sabbath.

As we can see, even if it were true that the New Testament does not repeat the command to observe the Sabbath, that still would not mean that the Sabbath is irrelevant for Christians. However, the New Testament *does*, in fact, reinforce Sabbath observance for Christians.

Can we observe any day of the week as the Sabbath?

The Sabbath is on the seventh day by definition. God did not sanctify any of the other days of the week. He sanctified the seventh day (Genesis 2:2-3). The seventh day of the week is the day we are commanded to observe as the Sabbath: "Six days you shall labor, and do all your work, but the seventh day is a Sabbath to the Lord your God" (Exodus 10:9-10).

Treating other days as the Sabbath is not fulfilling the instruction to observe the Sabbath because Scripture explicitly says to observe the seventh day. There is no biblical support for applying the characteristics of the Sabbath to days that are not the Sabbath. When Paul says, "One person esteems one day as better than another, while another esteems all days alike" and "each one should be fully convinced in his own mind" (Romans 14:5), he is not discussing the Sabbath but rather matters of personal "opinion" (Romans 14:1). Scripture never treats the Sabbath as a mere matter of opinion. As I covered in chapter 2,

---

38   Samuele Bacchiocchi, *The Sabbath in the New Testament* (Berrien Springs, MI: Biblical Perspectives, 2000), 50. Bacchiochi references Plutarch, *De Superstitione* 3 (Moralia 1660); Justin Martyr, *Dialogue with Trypho* 23, 3; Epiphanius, *Adversus Haereses* 30, 2, 2; *Apostolic Constitutions* 2, 36.

Paul is probably referring to traditional days for fasting in that verse. (Romans 14:6 indicates that one's observance or non-observance of the day is defined by their eating or abstaining—that is, whether or not they fast.)

Is it okay to go to church on Sunday if I still keep the Sabbath on the seventh day?

There is nothing wrong with attending church on Sunday (or any other day, for that matter). It would only be a problem if Sunday services became a replacement for Sabbath observance. As long as you observe the Sabbath on the seventh day per the commandment, attending church on other days of the week is not a problem.

What do Yeshua's Sabbath healings teach us about the Sabbath?

The gospels record several instances of Yeshua healing people on the Sabbath.[39] Should we interpret these Sabbath healings as evidence that Yeshua had come to do away with the Sabbath? According to John MacArthur, "Jesus appears to have chosen the Sabbath day for His healing purposely, because it struck a blow at this symbol. Jesus is announcing the end of the Sabbath."[40] I would agree with MacArthur that Yeshua chose the Sabbath for his healing miracles purposely. However, Yeshua's point was not to announce that the Sabbath was coming to an end. On the contrary, Yeshua's Sabbath healings demonstrate the proper way *to keep* the Sabbath. Like the Old Testament prophets, Yeshua condemns the misuse of the Sabbath day and calls God's people to observe the Sabbath according to its original purpose.

---

39   E.g., Mark 1:21-28; 29:31; 3:1-6; Luke 13:10-17; 14:1-6; John 5:1-18; 9:1-41.

40   John MacArthur, "Understanding the Sabbath," *Grace to You.* www.gty.org.

Let's consider one of the accounts of Yeshua healing someone on the Sabbath:

> Now he was teaching in one of the synagogues on the Sabbath. And behold, there was a woman who had had a disabling spirit for eighteen years. She was bent over and could not fully straighten herself. When Jesus saw her, he called her over and said to her, "Woman, you are freed from your disability." And he laid his hands on her, and immediately she was made straight, and she glorified God. But the ruler of the synagogue, indignant because Jesus had healed on the Sabbath, said to the people, "There are six days in which work ought to be done. Come on those days and be healed, and not on the Sabbath day." Then the Lord answered him, "You hypocrites! Does not each of you on the Sabbath untie his ox or his donkey from the manger and lead it away to water it? And ought not this woman, a daughter of Abraham whom Satan bound for eighteen years, be loosed from this bond on the Sabbath day?" As he said these things, all his adversaries were put to shame, and all the people rejoiced at all the glorious things that were done by him.
> —Luke 13:10-17

There are a couple of things worth pointing out here. First, the ruler of the synagogue interpreted Yeshua's healing as "work," and thus a violation of the Sabbath. Religious leaders accusing Yeshua of transgressing the Sabbath is a common theme in these healing accounts (Luke 6:6-11; John 5:16; 9:16). In one account, the Pharisees directly ask Yeshua if it is lawful to heal on the Sabbath. They asked this question for the sole purpose of having a reason to accuse Yeshua of wrongdoing

(Matthew 12:9-14). According to the later rabbinic literature, healing on the Sabbath was discouraged unless the illness was life-threatening (m. *Yoma* 8.6; m.*Shabbat* 14.3; 22:6). Based on what we see in the New Testament healing narratives, it seems like this was the perspective held by many of the religious leaders in Yeshua's time. However, the Torah itself does not prohibit healing or helping someone on the Sabbath. That is a man-made restriction.

The second thing worth pointing out is that Yeshua defends his actions, not by saying that the Sabbath no longer should be observed, but by explaining why his actions did not violate the Sabbath at all. He does this by employing a *kal v'chomer* argument. *Kal v'chomer* means "light and heavy," and it is the name of a principle for determining Torah application in Judaism. The basic idea is that if something applies in a less important case (a lighter matter), then it will also apply in a more important case (a heavier matter). Yeshua argues from a premise on which his audience would agree—in this case, that it is permissible to untie an ox or donkey on the Sabbath. From there, he concludes that it is obviously okay, therefore, to "untie" a woman from her disability on the Sabbath, since a daughter of Abraham is more important than an animal. He makes a similar argument in Matthew when he heals the man with the withered hand on the Sabbath:

> He said to them, "Which one of you who has a sheep, if it falls
> into a pit on the Sabbath, will not take hold of it and lift it
> out? Of how much more value is a man than a sheep! So it is
> lawful to do good on the Sabbath."
> —Matthew 12:11-12

If Yeshua was announcing the end of the Sabbath by healing people, his response to accusations that he violated the Sabbath seems strange. He literally makes a case for why his actions were *permissible*. Why did Yeshua defend his actions using a standard Jewish argument for determining Torah application if the Sabbath no longer mattered? Yeshua's response is simply not what we would expect from someone announcing the end of the Sabbath. But his response *is* what we would expect from someone who was correcting false doctrines and restoring the Sabbath's true purpose. And that is exactly what he seems to be doing.

Yeshua's teachings on the Sabbath closely resemble the teachings of the Old Testament Prophets. For example, consider the prophet Isaiah. Like some passages in the New Testament, some passages from the book of Isaiah could be misinterpreted as an attack on Sabbath observance if we miss the point of the message. Isaiah goes so far as to declare that God "hated" the Sabbath and feast days (Isaiah 1:13-14). Obviously, God does not actually hate his own holy days that he commanded his people to observe, just like he does not actually hate prayer (Isaiah 1:15). But he did hate it when his people prayed or observed these days while having corrupt hearts. In other words, he hates religious hypocrisy—that is, putting on an insincere religious show while disobeying God and neglecting to show love toward one's neighbor. This is why Isaiah's rebuke includes an appeal to repent and pursue justice:

> Wash yourselves; make yourselves clean; remove the evil of
> your deeds from before my eyes; cease to do evil, learn to do
> good; seek justice, correct oppression; bring justice to the
> fatherless, plead the widow's cause.
> —Isaiah 1:16-17

What good is Sabbath observance, prayer, singing worship songs, and making offerings at the Temple if it is all done without repentance? God rejects such expressions of worship when our hearts are far from him. From Isaiah's perspective, true worship, including Sabbath observance, must be done with a pure desire to love God and our neighbor, which is why Isaiah emphasizes seeking justice for others in his rebuke. But once again, Isaiah's emphasis on repentance and justice does not negate the importance of God's holy days. After all, elsewhere in Isaiah, the prophet admonishes God's people to *observe* the Sabbath (Isaiah 56:1-8; 58:13). His point is that acts of justice and righteousness *must accompany* our Sabbath observance:

> Thus says the Lord: "**Keep justice, and do righteousness**, for soon my salvation will come, and my righteousness be revealed. **Blessed is the man who does this**, and the son of man who holds it fast, **who keeps the Sabbath**, not profaning it, and keeps his hand from doing any evil."
> —Isaiah 56:1-2, emphasis added

Yeshua agreed with this sentiment wholeheartedly. In fact, that appears to be his entire point in these healing narratives. Yeshua's Sabbath observance included healing and ministering to the hurting and oppressed. And also like the Old Testament prophets, Yeshua constantly rebuked Israel's religious leaders for their hypocrisy. In Matthew 23, he condemns the Pharisees for neglecting what he calls the weightier matters of the Torah. But notice that he doesn't negate the lighter matters of the Torah in his emphasis of the weightier matters:

> Woe to you, scribes and Pharisees, hypocrites! For you tithe mint and dill and cumin, and have neglected the weightier

matters of the law: justice and mercy and faithfulness. These you ought to have done, **without neglecting the others**.
—Matthew 23:23, emphasis added

Like Isaiah, Yeshua taught that true Torah observance must be fueled by love for God and our neighbor. Otherwise, it is not genuine Torah observance. It is just a religious show. And that is what Yeshua's Sabbath healings were intended to announce—not an end to the Sabbath, but rather an end to religious hypocrisy. He calls for an end to neglecting those in our communities who are hurting. He says to stop turning the Sabbath day into a tool of oppression through anti-biblical, man-made restrictions.

Yeshua reminds us that the Sabbath is a day intended to bring rest and healing. It is a day made for man's benefit (Mark 2:27). And according to Yeshua, it is lawful to do good on the Sabbath (Matthew 12:12). In fact, doing good on the Sabbath is precisely what God expects of us. That is what the Sabbath is all about—it is a symbol of the ultimate rest and healing that we will enjoy in the world to come when God will wipe away every tear from our eyes and death and pain will be no more (Revelation 21:4). It is worth asking ourselves, "What am I doing to make sure my Sabbath rest reflects that future reality?" "What am I doing to wipe away the tears of those who are hurting in my community?" "What am I doing to ease the pain and suffering of others?" If we truly wish to honor the Sabbath, we ought to walk in the footsteps of our Savior and live out everything that this day is meant to symbolize.

The Sabbath is a ceremonial law, not a moral law. That means we don't have to keep it, right?

It has become popular in some circles to divide God's law (Torah) into categories called moral law (commands having to do with ethical actions toward God and others), civil law (commands having to do with theocratic Israelite society), and ceremonial law (commands having to do with religious ritual or ceremonies). According to this perspective, the ceremonial and civil parts of God's law are no longer relevant to Christians, but the moral parts of the law should still be kept. In this view, the Sabbath is usually categorized as part of the ceremonial law, and therefore, it does not apply to Christians. Here is John MacArthur articulating this view:

> You say, well, if the whole ceremonial law is now set aside,
> what's left? What's left is God and God's moral standards
> haven't changed... The ceremonial part of the law, gone. The
> moral part, which is the revelation of the character of God
> which has always been true, in all eras of redemptive history,
> is still in place and it is now clearly given to us on the pages of
> the Old Testament and the New Testament.[41]

There are problems with this argument. First, even if we grant the assumption that the Torah can be neatly categorized in this way, it still wouldn't follow that the "ceremonial" and "civil" parts of the Torah have passed away. Yeshua said that not an iota or dot would pass away from the Torah until heaven and earth pass away and all is accomplished—that is, until the end of the age (Matthew 5:18; cf. Revelation 21:1). Yeshua made no distinction. He didn't say that iotas

---

41   John MacArthur, "The Purpose of the Law," *Grace to You.* www.gty.org.

and dots from the ceremonial law will pass away at his death and resurrection. No, he said that not one iota or dot will pass away from the Torah. None of the commands from the Torah are "gone" according to Yeshua, regardless of which categories you place them in.

Second, the division of the Torah into these categories is utterly arbitrary and without biblical basis. The Scriptures themselves do not make such distinctions. When you read the Torah, all of the commandments are presented as a unified whole that reveals God's standards for how his people should live. For instance, Leviticus 19 starts with God's commandment to "be holy." The rest of the chapter defines what holiness looks like, giving commandments on everything from loving your neighbor as yourself (Leviticus 19:18) to being impartial in court (Leviticus 19:15) to keeping God's Sabbaths (Leviticus 19:3). *All* these commandments define holy conduct, and Christians must "be holy" according to what is "written" (1 Peter 1:14-16).

Third, many of God's commandments simply don't fit into any single category. The Sabbath is a great example. Many people would categorize it as "ceremonial," but it also has aspects that fit more with the civil and moral categories. For instance, profaning the Sabbath warranted the death penalty in ancient Israel (Exodus 31:14). Matters of capital punishment are traditionally designated as "civil law." Having the death penalty attached also places profaning the Sabbath on the same level as other sins that Christians normally see as serious moral issues (murder, blasphemy, homosexual behavior, sorcery, etc.). Moreover, in the quote above, MacArthur defines moral law as that which reveals God's character. For instance, "love your neighbor" is part of the moral law. We must obey the command to love our neighbor because God loves, and loving our neighbor makes us more like him. But God also rested on the Sabbath (Genesis 2:2-3). Thus, resting on the Sabbath is doing what God did, making us more like him.

Much more could be said about these arbitrary categories that people try to force the Torah into.[42] However, regardless of whether you label it ceremonial, moral, or civil, Scripture is clear that the Sabbath is important, and God expects his people to observe it.

Is keeping the Sabbath a salvation issue?

We are saved only by grace through faith (Ephesians 2:8). Nothing we do could ever earn salvation. It is a gift of God. We obey God not to be saved but because we are saved.

The Sabbath does not play a part in our salvation, but it should play a part in our obedience as Christians. As Christians, we believe in keeping plenty of commandments (honoring parents, tithing, caring for the poor, etc.), and none of those things are done in order to "be saved." The Sabbath is a biblical commandment like any of the other commandments that Christians routinely observe. It is one of the commandments that Yeshua tells us to do and teach (Matthew 5:19). Christians who have recognized that the Sabbath is still relevant for today should *want* to honor it as an expression of their love for God. Observing the Sabbath does not grant salvation, but it is part of the Christian's loving response to the salvation they have already received.

We are not "under the law." Does that mean we are freed from having to observe the Sabbath?

Romans 6:14 says, "For sin will have no dominion over you, since you are not under law but under grace." Some have interpreted this verse as exempting believers from obedience to God's law (Torah), including the Sabbath. It is said that not being "under the law" means being freed from one's obligation to obey it.

---

42   See Tim Hegg, *Why We Keep Torah*, 133-142.

However, this interpretation has problems. First, it clearly contradicts Paul's numerous pro-Torah statements within Romans itself. Paul declares that our faith does not overthrow the Torah, but rather establishes it (Romans 3:31). He teaches that sin is defined as breaking the Torah's commandments (Romans 7:7) and admonishes believers not to continue living in sin (Romans 6:1-2). He calls the Torah holy, righteous, and good (Romans 7:12). He calls the Torah spiritual (Romans 7:14) and says he delights in it (Romans 7:22). He says the Holy Spirit empowers believers to keep the Torah (Romans 8:2-4).

Second, the immediate context precludes the interpretation that being "not under law" means "freed from having to keep it." The next verse says, "What then? Are we to sin because we are not under law but under grace? By no means" (Romans 6:15)! That is, being under grace *does not* give us freedom to sin. What is sin? Breaking the Torah's commandments (Romans 7:7). Indeed, if "not under law" means "freed from having to keep the law," then Paul's statement in Romans 6:15 makes no sense.

If "not under law" does not mean freed from one's obligation to keep the law, then what *does* it mean? The scholar Charles E. B. Cranfield provides a much more coherent interpretation:

> [This phrase] is widely taken to mean that the authority of
> the law has been abolished for believers and superseded by a
> different authority. And this, it must be admitted, would be
> a plausible interpretation, if this sentence stood by itself. But,
> since it stands in a document which contains such things as
> 3:31; 7;12, 14a; 8:4; 13:8-10, and in which the law is referred
> to more than once as God's law (7:22, 25; 8:7) and is appealed
> to again and again as authoritative, such a reading of it is
> extremely unlikely. The fact that "under law" is contrasted with

"under grace" suggests the likelihood that Paul is here thinking not of the law generally but of the law as condemning sinners; for, since grace denotes God's undeserved favour, the natural opposite to "under grace" is "under God's disfavour or condemnation." And the suggestion that the meaning of this sentence is that believers are not under God's condemnation pronounced by the law but under His undeserved favour receives strong confirmation from 8:1 ("There is therefore now no condemnation to those who are in Christ Jesus"), which, in Paul's argument, is closely related (through 7:1-6) to this half-verse. Moreover, this interpretation suits the context well; for an assurance that we have been set free from God's condemnation and are now the objects of His gracious favour is indeed confirmation ("for") of the promise that henceforth sin shall no more be lord over us, for those who know themselves freed from condemnation are free to resist sin's usurped power with new strength and boldness.[43]

As Cranfield notes, in Romans 6:14, Paul is "not thinking of the law generally but of the law as condemnation for sinners." In other words, when Paul says that we are not under the law, what he means is that we are not under condemnation for breaking the law. Instead, we who are in Messiah are forgiven and under grace. The Messiah took upon himself the punishment due to us for our sin, freeing us from sin's dominion: "There is therefore now no condemnation for those who are in Christ Jesus" (Romans 8:1). But again, being under grace

---

43   Charles E. B. Cranfield, *The Epistle to the Romans* (T&T Clark, 1975), 1.305.

does not give us license to break the Torah's commandments, including the Sabbath (Romans 6:15).[44]

How should Sabbath observers interact with other Christians who don't observe the Sabbath?

All genuine Christians, whether they observe the Sabbath or not, are brothers and sisters. I do not believe it is right to divide from other genuine Christians over this issue. Genuine Christians who don't observe the Sabbath will not divide from Sabbath observers over this issue either, as long as the Sabbath observers are not causing actual problems (like gossiping or sowing discord). If a group tells a Sabbath observer that he is no longer saved, or that he must cease from observing the Sabbath in order to maintain fellowship with the group, then, unfortunately, separation will become necessary. However, usually it takes more than the mere fact that a Christian is resting on the seventh day to get him disinvited from fellowship.

The bottom line is that all genuine Christians affirm the essential doctrines of Christianity. We can worship together, partner together in evangelism, and stand firm together on biblical morality in the face of an increasingly hostile and immoral secular world. However, the Sabbath is an important commandment that has largely been forgotten in Christianity. As Christians who have come to realize the joy and importance of the Sabbath, we should want other Christians to receive this blessing as well. We should certainly seek to persuade other Christians from the Scriptures that the Sabbath is for today.

---

44 For more on the phrase "under the law" in the New Testamnet, see Hegg, *Why We Keep Torah*, 75-89; J.K. McKee, *The New Testament Validates Torah* (Richardson, TX: Messianic Apologetics, 2012), 295-335.

However, it is not our place to look down on other Christians who don't observe the Sabbath. This revelation that we have been given is ultimately a gracious gift from God. We are no better or more special than anyone else. We must walk out God's commandments, including the Sabbath, in humility and gratitude, not pride and self-righteousness. When we do that, then maybe those we hope to influence will see the value in Sabbath observance because they will see the good fruit it has produced in our lives.

CHAPTER 6
CONCLUSION

What does the New Testament say about Sabbath observance for Christians? Here is what we have learned:

The New Testament affirms the Sabbath's enduring validity

We saw that Yeshua affirmed the Sabbath's enduring validity in Matthew 5:17-20. Yeshua said he came to fulfill the Torah—that is, confirm the Torah through his teachings and actions, demonstrating how to observe it properly. Nothing from the Torah will pass away until the future consummation of the kingdom when heaven and earth pass away. Followers of Yeshua are to do and teach even the least of the Torah's commandments in accordance with Yeshua's teachings, thereby surpassing the scribes and Pharisees in righteousness. The Torah includes the command to observe the Sabbath.

In Mark 2:27, we saw that Yeshua expressed the Sabbath's universal and perpetual nature when he said that the Sabbath was established in creation for all mankind. Yeshua's statement on the Sabbath's purpose implies that it is still relevant to all Christians today.

In the book of Acts, we learned that the apostles observed the Sabbath and expected even new Gentile converts to observe it too. Thirty years after Yeshua's earthly ministry, "thousands" of Jerusalem Christians were still zealous for the Torah and still keeping the Sabbath. Paul went to some length to reassure these Christians that the rumors about him were false and that he also lived in accordance with the Torah, which is what we would expect from someone who affirmed the ongoing validity of the Sabbath.

Additionally, when we examined writings from Paul, Peter, John, James, and Hebrews, we saw that they contained instructions indicating that the Sabbath is still relevant to Christians. The Sabbath is part of the Torah that Paul says the Holy Spirit empowers us to keep. Peter says that Christians must be holy in all our conduct, and keeping the Sabbath is part of what defines holy conduct. John says that genuine Christians will keep God's commandments, which undoubtedly includes the commandment to keep the Sabbath. James says that Christians must be "doers of the word," which implies Sabbath observance. Finally, the author of Hebrews indicates that Sabbath observance is still relevant to God's people.

The Sabbath was not repealed

In Matthew 12:1-8, we saw that Yeshua's confrontation with the Pharisees was over how to keep the Sabbath, not an example of Yeshua disregarding the Sabbath. Yeshua defended his disciples against the Pharisees' accusation that they broke the Sabbath and asserted his authority as the rightful interpreter of the commandment.

In Colossians 2:16-17, Paul did not condemn biblical Sabbath observance but only a misuse of the Sabbath and festivals in connection with mystical false teachings. The problem in Colossae was human precepts and teachings, not God's commandments themselves (Colossians 2:8, 22). When commandments like the Sabbath are honored appropriately, focusing on the Messiah and his work of redemption, there is no problem.

In Romans 14, we saw that the conflict over days and foods that Paul addresses in the chapter had nothing to do with the Sabbath and dietary laws in the Torah. The controversy had to do with man's opinions over ritual purity and designated fast days. Since the issues in

Rome did not concern obedience to the clear commands of Scripture, Paul advises people on both sides to tolerate each other's opinions.

In Galatians 4:10, we learned that Paul's mention of "days and months and seasons and years" refers to pagan festival observances, not biblical holy days like the Sabbath. Paul's concern was that his readers, who were former pagans, might "turn back again" to these pagan observances because they were led to believe that returning to paganism was their only option if they refused to convert to Judaism. Paul addresses this false choice presented to his readers by emphasizing the true gospel, which teaches that the Gentile believers are already full members of God's family by virtue of their faith in the Messiah. Having refuted the idea that the Gentile believers must "convert or leave," in Galatians 4:8-11, Paul admonishes them not to return to paganism.

In Hebrews 4:9, we saw that the author does not indicate that Sabbath observance had been nullified in light of the Sabbath's deeper meaning. After all, nobody believes that Yeshua's teachings on the deeper meanings of the commandments against murder and adultery did away with those literal commandments, or that Paul's teaching on the deeper meaning of marriage did away with the literal marriage institution. Instead, the Greek word for "Sabbath rest" actually suggests that literal Sabbath observance "remains" for God's people. As Christians, our Sabbath observance should remind us of the eternal rest we have in the Messiah.

Sunday did not replace the Sabbath

Looking at the New Testament, we saw that the earliest Christians continued to keep the Sabbath in accordance with the biblical commandment. The New Testament references to the first day of the week do not establish weekly Sunday meetings and certainly do not support a replacement of the Sabbath with Sunday.

Looking at the early centuries after the apostles' time, we saw that Christians did not universally reject Sabbath observance. Most Christians observed both the Sabbath and Sunday as late as the fifth century. The decline of Sabbath observance and the rise of exclusive Sunday observance in early Christianity emerged first in Alexandria and Rome and was largely motived by anti-Jewish sentiment. Nevertheless, Sunday was not considered a day of rest until 321 A.D., when Constantine decreed that Sunday be a day of rest. This edict started the long process of Christians assigning to Sunday the characteristics of the Sabbath commandment. However, Scripture nowhere endorses this change.

The Sabbath is for both Jewish and Gentile believers

Looking at Scripture, we learned that the idea that the Sabbath is only for Jews and not Gentiles is without biblical basis. Several Old and New Testament passages testify that the Sabbath commandment applies to both Jewish and Gentile believers. The apostles were to teach "all the nations" Yeshua's commandments (Matthew 28:19-20), which would have included his instructions to observe even the least of the Torah's commandments (Matthew 5:17-20). Furthermore, according to Yeshua, the Sabbath was established in the beginning for the benefit of all mankind, so it was never intended to be an exclusively Jewish institution (Mark 2:27). This aligns with Old Testament teaching that explicitly calls for Gentiles who have embraced Israel's God to observe the Sabbath.

In Acts 15, we saw that the apostles did not exempt Gentile believers from laws like the Sabbath. In reality, this passage addresses the separate issue of ritual conversion for salvation. The apostles taught that Gentile believers did not need to convert to Judaism to be saved and received into the community. Still, it was assumed that the Gentile believers would continue to learn the Torah every Sabbath as they attended synagogue services.

Looking at what Scripture says about the New Covenant, we saw that the Sabbath remains valid for Christians. Once again, the Sabbath was given to all mankind at the beginning, long before the covenant was made with Israel at Mount Sinai. Further, believing Gentiles are part of the commonwealth of Israel and the New Covenant writes the Torah (including the Sabbath) on the hearts of believers, including Gentile believers.

Based on our study of the New Testament's teaching on the topic of Sabbath observance, it is clear that we should honor the Sabbath as Christians. The Sabbath, God's day of rest, is a gift to mankind. Will you receive it?

BIBLIOGRAPHY

Arnold, Clinton E. *The Colossian Syncretism: The Interface between Christianity and Folk Belief at Colossae.* Grand Rapids, MI: Baker Books, 1996.

Bacchiocchi, Samuele. *From Sabbath to Sunday: A Historical Investigation of the Rise of Sunday Observance in Early Christianity.* Rome, Italy: The Pontifical Gregorian University Press, 1977.

Bacchiocchi, Samuele. "The Rise of Sunday Observance in Early Christianity." *The Sabbath in Scripture and History*, Kenneth Strand, ed. Washington: Review and Herald Publishing, 1982.

Bacchiocchi, Samuele. *The Sabbath in the New Testament.* Berrien Springs, MI: Biblical Perspectives, 2000.

Bauckham, Richard. "The Lord's Day." *From Sabbath to Lord's Day: A Biblical, Historical and Theological Investigation*, D.A. Carson, ed. Grand Rapids, MI: Zondervan, 1982.

Bauer, Walter. *A Greek-English Lexicon of the New Testament and Other Early Christian Literature*, rev. and ed. Frederick W. Danker, 4th ed. Chicago: University of Chicago Press, 2021.

Beckwith, Roger T. *Calendar and Chronology, Jewish and Christian: Biblical, Intertestamental and Patristic Studies.* Brill Academic Publishers, 2001.

Brown, Francis, Driver, S., Briggs, C. *Hebrew and English Lexicon of the Old Testament.* Oxford: Clarendon Press, 1979.

Bruce, F. F. *1 and 2 Corinthians.* London: Oliphants, 1971.

Bruce, F. F. *The Book of the Acts.* Grand Rapids, MI: Eerdmans, 1988.

Bruce, F.F. *Colossians, Philemon, Ephesians.* Grand Rapids, MI: Eerdmans, 1984.

Christian, Ed. "Sabbath Is a Happy Day! What Does Isaiah 58:13-14 Mean?" *JATS* 13/1 (Spring 2002): 81-90.

Cohen, Shaye J. D. *The beginnings of Jewishness: Boundaries, Varieties, Uncertainties.* Los Angeles: University of California Press, 1999.

Cole, R. Alan. *Exodus.* Downers Grove, IL: InterVarsity Press, 2016.

Cranfield, Charles E. B. *The Epistle to the Romans.* T&T Clark, 1975.

Dart, Ronald L. "Examining arguments for and against the Sabbath," *Pro Torah.* https://www.protorah.com/examining-arguments-for-and-against-the-sabbath/.

Donaldson, Terence L. *Paul and the Gentiles: Remapping the Apostle's Convictional World.* Minneapolis: Fortress Press, 2006.

Dunn, James. *The New Perspective on Paul.* Grand Rapids: Eerdmans, 2008.

Enns, Peter. *Exodus.* Grand Rapids, MI: Zondervan 2000.

Evans, Craig A. *Matthew.* Cambridge University Press, 2012.

Fortin, Denis. "Paul's Observance of the Sabbath in Acts of the Apostles as a Marker of Continuity Between Judaism and Early Christianity." *AUSS* Vol. 40, No. 2 (2015): 321-335.

Gane, Roy. "Sabbath and the New Covenant." *JATS,* 10/1-2 (1999): 311-332

Geraty, Lawrence T. "From Sabbath to Sunday: Why, How and When?" *Partings: How Judaism and Christianity Became Two,* Hershel Shanks, ed. Washington, DC: Biblical Archaeology Society, 2013.

Gingrich, F. W. *Shorter Lexicon of the Greek New Testament.* Chicago, IL: University of Chicago Press, 1965.

González, Justo L. *A Brief History of Sunday: From the New Testament to the New Creation.* Grand Rapids, MI: Wm. B. Eerdmans Publishing Co., 2017.

Gupta, Nijay K. *Colossians.* Macon, GA: Smyth and Helwys, 2013.

Guttmann, Alexander. "The End of the Sacrificial Jewish Cult" *HUCA* 38, 1967.

Hagner, Donald A. *Matthew 1-13: Word Biblical Commentary 33a.* Dallas, TX: Word, 1993.

Hagner, Donald A. *Matthew 14-28: Word Biblical Commentary 33b.* Dallas, TX: Word, 1995.

Harris, R. Laird, Archer, Gleason L., Waltke, Bruce K. *Theological Wordbook of the Old Testament.* Chicago: Moody Press, 1980.

Hartin, P.J. "Ethics in the Letter of James, the Gospel of Matthew, and the Didache: Their Place in Early Christian Literature." *Matthew, James, and Didache: Three Related Documents in Their Jewish and Christian Settings.* Atlanta, GA: Society of Biblical Literature, 2008.

Hegg, Caleb. *Instruction for Community, Family, & Personal Living: A Commentary on Colossians & Philemon.* Growing in Messiah, 2021.

Hegg, Tim. *A Commentary on The Book of Hebrews Chapters 1-8.* Tacoma, WA: TorahResource, 2016.

Hegg, Tim. *A Commentary on the Epistle of James.* Tacoma, WA: TorahResource, 2021.

Hegg, Tim. *Paul's Epistle to the Galatians.* Tacoma, WA: TorahResource, 2010.

Hegg, Tim. *Paul's Epistle to the Romans: Chapters 9-16.* Tacoma, WA: TorahResource, 2007.

Hegg, Tim, *The Gospel of Matthew: Chapters 1-7.* Tacoma, WA: TorahResource, 2007.

Hegg, Tim, *The Gospel of Matthew: Chapters 24-28.* Tacoma, WA: TorahResource, 2013.

Hegg, Tim. "What Does Plerosai ('to fulfill') Mean in Matthew 5:17?" *ETS Annual Meeting.* Nashville, 2000.

Hegg, Tim. *Why We Keep Torah: 10 Persistent Questions*. Tacoma, WA: TorahResource, 2009.

House, Colin. "Defilement by Association: Some Insights From the usage of KOINOS/KOINOU in Acts 10 and 11." *AUSS* (1983), Vol. 21, No. 2: 143-153.

Hyatt, J.P. *Exodus*. New Century Bible, 1971.

Imes, Carmen. *Bearing God's Name: Why Sinai Still Matters*. Downer's Grove, IL: InterVarsity Press, 2019.

Janicki, Toby. *The Didache: A New Translation and Messianic Jewish Commentary*. Marshfield, MO: Vine of David, 2017.

Keener, Craig. *Acts: An Exegetical Commentary, 3:1-14:28*. Grand Rapids: BakerAcademic, 2013.

Keener, Craig. *Acts: An Exegetical Commentary, 15:1-23:35*. Grand Rapids, MI: Baker Academic, 2014.

Keener, Craig. *Acts: New Cambridge Bible Commentary*. United Kingdom: Cambridge University Press, 2020.

Keener, Craig. *New Cambridge Bible Commentary: Galatians*. Cambridge University Press, 2018.

Keener, Craig. *NIV Cultural Backgrounds Study Bible: Bringing to Life the Ancient World of Scripture*. Grand Rapids, MI: Zondervan, 2016.

Keener, Craig. *The Gospel of Matthew: A Socio-Rhetorical Commentary*. Grand Rapids, MI: Eerdmans, 1999.

Keener, Craig. "Which day is the Sabbath?" *Bible Background: Research and Commentary from Dr. Craig Keener*. https://craigkeener.com/which-day-is-the-sabbath/.

Kistemaker, Simon J. *Exposition of the Epistle of the Hebrews*. Grand Rapids, MI: Baker, 1984.

Kraft, Robert A. "Sabbath in Early Christianity," *AUSS*. Andrews University Press, 1965.

Lancaster, D. Thomas. *From Sabbath to Sabbath: Returning the Holy Sabbath to the Disciples of Jesus.* Marshfield, MO: First Fruits of Zion, 2016.

Lancaster, D. Thomas. *Torah Club: Chronicles of the Apostles.* Marshfield, MO: First Fruits of Zion, 2012.

Lewis, Richard B. "Ignatius and the 'Lord's Day.'" *AUSS* 6.1 (1968): 45-59.

Liddell, H.G., Scott, R. *A Greek-English Lexicon.* Oxford: Clarendon Press, 1996.

Liefeld, Walter L. *1 & 2 Timothy, Titus.* Grand Rapids, MI: Zondervan, 1999.

Lincoln, A. T. *Colossians: New Interpreters Bible,* Vol. 11. Abington Press, 2000.

Lincoln, A.T. *Ephesians: Word Biblical Commentary 42.* Grand Rapids, MI: Zondervan, 1990.

Lincoln, A.T. "Sabbath, Rest, and Eschatology in the New Testament." *From Sabbath to Lord's Day: A Biblical, Historical, and Theological Investigation.* Grand Rapids, MI: Zondervan, 1982.

MacArthur, John. "Is the Sabbath for Today?" *Grace to You.* https://www.gty.org/library/bibleqnas-library/QA0294/is-the-sabbath-for-today.

MacArthur, John. "Receiving One Another with Understanding, Part 2." *Grace to You.* https://www.gty.org/library/sermons-library/45-109/receiving-one-another-with-understanding-part-2.

MacArthur, John. "The Purpose of the Law," *Grace to You.* https://www.gty.org/library/sermons-library/80-178/the-purpose-of-the-law.

MacArthur, John. "Understanding the Sabbath." *Grace to You.* https://www.gty.org/library/sermons-library/90-379/understanding-the-sabbath.

MacArthur, John. "Why Sunday is the Lord's Day," *Grace to You.* https://www.gty.org/library/sermons-library/90-380/why-sunday-is-the-lords-day.

MacCarty, Skip. "The Seventh-Day Sabbath." *Perspectives on the Sabbath: 4 Views*, Christopher Donato, ed. Nashville, TN: B& H Academic, 2011.

Marshall, I. Howard. *Luke* (Grand Rapids, MI: Eerdmans Publishing, 1978.

Martin, Troy. "Pagan and Judeo-Christian Time-Keeping Schemes in Gal 4.10 and Col 2.16." *New Testament Studies* 42 (1996): 105-119.

McIver, Robert K. "When, where, and why did the change from Sabbath to Sunday worship take place in the early church?" *AUSS* 53 (2015): 15-35.

McKee, J. K. *Acts 15 For The Practical Messianic*. McKinney, TX: Messianic Apologetics, 2010.

McKee, J. K. *Messianic Sabbath Helper*, Margaret Huey, ed. McKinney, TX: Messianic Apologetics, 2015.

McKee, J. K. *The New Testament Validates Torah: Does the New Testament Really Do Away With the Law?* Richardson, TX: Messianic Apologetics, 2012.

McKnight, Scot. *The New International Commentary of the New Testament: The Letter of James.* Grand Rapids, MI: Eerdmans, 2011.

Metzger, Bruce M. *Studies in Lectionary Text of the Greek New Testament.* Chicago, IL: University of Chicago Press, 1944.

Milavec, Aaron. *The Didache: Faith, Hope, & Life of the Earliest Christian Communities, 50-70 C.E.* New York, NY: Newman, 2003.

Moo, Douglas. *Pillar New Testament Commentary: The Letters to the Colossians and to Philemon.* Grand Rapids, MI: Eerdmans, 2008.

Nolland, John, *The Gospel of Matthew*. United Kingdom: Eerdmans Publishing Company, 2005.

O'Brien, Peter T. *Word Biblical Commentary: Colossians, Philemon*. Nashville, TN: Thomas Nelson, 1982.

Overman, J. Andrew. *Church and Community in Crisis: The Gospel According to Matthew*. Valley Forge, PA: Trinity Press International.

Overman, J. Andrew. *Matthew's Gospel and Formative Judaism: The Social World of the Matthean Community*. Minneapolis, MN: Fortress Press, 1990.

Patzia, Arthur G. *The Emergence of the Church: Context, Growth, Leadership and Worship*. Downers Grove, IL: InterVarsity Press, 2001.

Pritz, Ray A. *Nazarene Jewish Christianity: From the End of the New Testament Period Until Its Disappearance in the Fourth Century*. The Hebrew University, Jerusalem: The Magnes Press, 1988.

Rabinowits, Noel. "Yes, the Torah is Fulfilled, But What Does This Mean?: An Exegetical Exposition." *Kesher* 11 (2000): 19-44.

Richardson, Cyril C. *Early Christian Fathers*. Louisville, KY: The Westminster Press, 1953.

Robertson, O. Palmer. *The Christ of the Covenants*. Phillipsburg, NJ: Presbyterian and Reformed Publishing, 1980.

Rodríguez, A. M. "The Biblical Sabbath: The Adventist Perspective." *Biblical Research Institute General Conference of Seventh-day Adventists* (2002).

Sanders, E. P. *Jewish Law from Jesus to the Mishnah*. Philadelphia, PA: Trinity Press International, 1990.

Schaff, Philip. *History of the Christian Church*. New York: Thomas Y. Crowell, 1894.

Scherman, Nosson. *ArtScroll Chumash*, Stone Edition. Brooklyn: Mesorah Publications, Ltd., 2000.

Schumacher, Andrew. "Matthew 5 and the Hebrew Roots Movement." *Beginning of Wisdom.* https://beginningwisdom.org/matthew-5-and-the-hebrew-roots-movement/.

Shea, William. "The Sabbath in Matthew 24:20." *AUSS* 40 (2002): 23-35.

Skarsaune, Oskar. *In the Shadow of the Temple: Jewish Influences on Early Christianity.* Downers Grove, IL: IVP Academic, 2002.

Smith, T. C. *Acts: The Broadman Bible Commentary.* Nashville, TN: 1970.

Solberg, R. L. *Torahism: Are Christians Required to Keep the Law of Moses?* Williamson College Press, 2019.

Specht, Walter F. "The Sabbath in the New Testament." *The Sabbath in Scripture and History*, Kenneth A. Strand, ed. Washington, DC: Review and Herald, 1982.

Spurgeon, Charles H. "God's Law in Man's Heart." *The Spurgeon Center.* https://www.spurgeon.org/resource-library/sermons/gods-law-in-mans-heart/#flipbook/.

Stanley, Andy. *Irresistible: Reclaiming the New that Jesus Unleashed for the World.* Grand Rapids, MI: Zondervan, 2018.

Stefanovic, Ranko. "The Lord's Day of Revelation 1:10 in the Current Debate." *AUSS* 49 (2011): 261-284.

Strand, Kenneth A. "Another Look at 'Lord's Day' in the Early Church and in Rev. i. 10." *New Testament Studies* 13 (1967): 174-182.

Strand, Kenneth A. "The 'Lord's Day' in the Second Century." *The Sabbath in Scripture and History*, Kenneth Strand, ed. Washington: Review and Herald Publishing, 1982.

Strand, Kenneth A. "The Sabbath and Sunday From the Second Through Fifth Centuries." *The Sabbath in Scripture and History.* Washington, D.C.: Review and Herald Publishing., 1982.

Stuart, Douglas K. *Exodus*. Nashville: B&H Publishing Group, 2006.

Thiessen, Matthew. "Abolishers of the Law in Early Judaism and Matthew 5,17-20." *Biblica* 93, no 4 (2012): 543-56.

Thiessen, Matthew. "Hebrews and the Jewish Law." *So Great A Salvation: A Dialogue on the Atonement in Hebrews*, ed. Jon C. Laansma, George H. Guthrie, and Cynthia Westfall. London: T&T Clark, 2019.

Thiessen, Matthew. *Jesus and the Forces of Death: The Gospels' Portrayal of Ritual Impurity Within First-Century Judaism*. Grand Rapids, MI: BakerAcademic, 2020.

Tigay, Jeffrey. *Deuteronomy*. Jerusalem: The Jewish Publican Society, 1996.

Turner, David L. *Matthew*. Grand Rapids, MI: Baker Academic, 2008.

Vines, Matthew. *God and the Gay Christian: The Biblical Case in Support of Same-Sex Relationships*. Convergent Books, 2014.

Wahlen, Clinton. "Peter's Vision and Conflicting Definitions of Purity." *NTS* 51 (2005).

Walker, Alexander. *Ante-Nicene Fathers*, Vol. 8. Alexander Roberts, James Donaldson, and A. Cleveland Coxe, ed. Buffalo, NY: Christian Literature Publishing Co., 1886.

Watson, R.L. *Forgotten Covenant*. Port Orchard, WA: Ark House Press, 2021.

Weiss, Herold. *A Day of Gladness: The Sabbath among Jews and Christians in Antiquity*. Columbia, SC: University of South Carolina Press, 2003.

Witherington III, Ben. *The Acts of the Apostles: A Socio-Rhetorical Commentary*. Grand Rapids, MI: Eerdmans, 1998.

Woolvard, John. *The Revelation of Jesus Christ*. Moody Press, 1966.

Young, Norman H. "The Use of Sunday for Meetings of Believers in the New Testament': A Response." *Novum Testamentum* 45 (2003): 111-122.

Made in the USA
Las Vegas, NV
07 October 2023

78756457R10115